Decolonising design education
edited by the Bauhaus Dessau Foundation
(Regina Bittner, Katja Klaus, Philipp Sack)
and Gudskul (JJ Adibrata, farid rakun)

Schools of Departure No. 1

T0028718

Article	Title/Author	Page

Table of Contents

Table of Contents

Table of Contents

Table of Contents

Travelling concepts beyond the Bauhaus

1

The study collection of the National Institute of Design (NID) in Ahmedabad gathers 20th-century design objects that do not fit into a linear narrative of western design history defined by characteristics of style. Fragments of Marcel Breuer's B3 chair are found alongside MP Rajan's Bamboo Cube, an object that he designed with students in collaboration with rural craft communities. Chairs by the Japanese-American designer George Nakashima, who taught at the NID and drew on Asian seating traditions and materials, are juxtaposed with furniture by Gajanan Upadhyaya, who likewise taught at the NID. Some of these pieces point to a collaboration with Hans Gugelot from the Ulm School of Design, who briefly taught in Ahmedabad. Chairs by Charles and Ray Eames, Ludwig Mies van der Rohe and Alvar Aalto are also present. In the wall cabinets there are stacks of baskets and pottery water containers collected by students of the NID in so-called craft documentations excursions supposed to engage students with rural craft traditions. The collection of western prototypes mixed with other objects originated from a travelling exhibition curated by New York's Museum of Modern Art (MoMA) which toured several Indian cities from 1959. This exhibition titled *Design Today in America and Europe* is not merely a typical example of American cultural diplomacy during the Cold War; it also promoted the notion of 'good design' firmly linked with capitalist industrialisation and modernisation according to a western model, with 'machine-made' product design and commodity aesthetics being its central features. Thus, while the exhibition showcased design achievements of the western world, it also served the purpose of 'teaching' the message of 'good design' to a non-western public. After the exhibition had toured for two years, the objects were handed over to the newly founded National Institute of Design, the design school of a modern India. The fact that this collection of prototypes has not been taken over in its pure form— that is, as a display of functional, capitalist-industrial mass products of highly technological processes— may be traced back to the controversies on how to reassess the profession of the designer that began with the founding of the NID, with profound geopolitical and social-environmental transitions as a backdrop. Singanapalli Balaram, a former tutor at the NID, had attested to a deep crisis in the "modern movement, the reductionist, the rationalist and mechanist-type design movement". With his 'Barefoot Designer' programme, he proposed places of learning in rural locations for a collective design practice in step with local conditions of production and making.[1] This strand of postcolonial design discourse culminated in the 1979 international conference *Design for Development* at the NID, which aimed to step away from hegemonial western design paradigms. International organisations such as the International Council of Societies of Industrial Design (ICSID) and the United Nations Industrial Development Organization (UNIDO), which arranged these conferences, exhibited an understanding of design firmly rooted in a development paradigm. However, at the same time, these conferences offered platforms for the critical examination of questions of environment and design in the Global South. Facing the West's often-reductionist attempts at exporting its modernisation models, several developing nations sought alternative practices for both economic and social change. In Ahmedabad, the international delegates argued in support of a postcolonial understanding of design, expressing a desire to disengage from the western hegemony that associated design with formal aesthetic ideals and universalistic claims to validity. According to design historian Alison J. Clarke, the ensuing *Ahmedabad Declaration* came out in favour of "design as a tool for social change within a humanist paradigm that crossed both post-industrial and so-called developing nations."[2] This, Clarke argues, represented the emergence of "an alternative design movement underpinned by theories of anthropology, intermediate technology, development studies and neo-Marxist critique of Western consumer culture."[3]

Why does the NID teaching collection appear to offer a suitable critical framework for a book discussing facets of the decolonisation of education? Firstly, an inventory of the collection, which emerged in the context of diverse learning experiments, production practices and design schools, contradicts any attempt at summarising the history of design in a linear narrative. These linear historiographies associated the discipline with western urbanisation and capitalist industrialisation, which frequently finds a starting or reference point in the historical Bauhaus. Written from the dominant perspective of western modernism perceived as universal, such narratives ignore its complicity in colonial exploitation, environmental destruction, extractivism, and epistemological hegemony. More-over, these historiographies mostly take on an implicit male-centred perspective. Such narratives, which continue to dominate design education, must be countered by narratives and histories that describe this as a diverse field of collaborative and conflictual practices involving various actors, economies, materials, knowledge types, and technologies, and simultaneously acknowledge the way this field is shaped by power structures, asymmetries and inequalities.

Secondly, the collection's dis-order conjures unexpected conversations around the objects, engendering speculative approaches to and redefinitions of design activity, learning and knowledge. Ultimately, discourses on the decolonisation of design also propose a new ontological perspective on the activity of design in the light of challenges threatening the entire planet. Here, design is no longer understood as a mode of action supporting the binary division between a passive, malleable, voiceless material to be shaped by the human hand, and an autonomous cultural superiority of the world of ideas, forms and meanings. The baskets in the NIDs study collection are thus witnesses of an alternative approach to design knowledge and activity. Tim Ingold extrapolates this new perspective from the practice of basket weaving: forms, he suggests, "are not imposed from above but grow from the mutual involvement of people and materials".[4] This radical ontological transformation strives to overcome the inherent anthropocentricity of western design theory, and in doing so calls for a learning of indigenous, non-western epistemologies. The idea that any problem is best approached following the paradigms of resolvability and feasibility is replaced by a practice of design conceptualised a continual process of co-habitation, co-constitution and becoming, as a reciprocal relation between multiple species.

From this, we arrive at the third aspect of the practices and epistemologies of decolonisation central to this book. Decolonial thought, as Ramón Grosfoguel suggests, projects "a pluriversal as opposed to a universal world" which develops in "critical dialogue between diverse critical epistemic/ethical/political projects".[5] Associated with this is the call to no longer consider design as universally valid, but as a situated mode of action and thought. Arturo Escobar speaks of "multiple transition narratives and forms of activism [...] veritable cultural and ecological transitions to different societal models going beyond strategies that offer anthropocene conditions as solutions".[6] Places of learning and initiatives for cooperative and supportive action emerge as "minor gestures" of structural transition in a variety of local projects, especially in South America and Southeast Asia.[7]

1   The thoughts outlined above prompt the following question: can a journal whose frame of reference is situated in the educational legacy of the historical Bauhaus—a problematic legacy deeply intertwined with the modernist tradition—contribute at all to the project of decolonising design? Can we offer a way forward that is conscious of the epistemological and practical necessity of scrutinising the modernist tradition, but without utterly disregarding the connection we have with it?

In this series, the pedagogical approaches associated with the Bauhaus are not understood as a legacy in the sense of a tradition perpetuating itself, which revolves around the notion of an 'original' Bauhaus. Rather, the volumes published in the series draw on notions such as 'travelling concepts' and 'translation'. Learning experiments, ideas, materials, narratives, and radical educational media move through time and space; however, this journey does not follow the linear notion claiming that these ideas are universally valid. Of interest here are the complicated and often bumpy paths of translation processes that, as Walter Benjamin proposed in his essay *The Task of the Translator*, only coincide with the original "just as a tangent touches a circle lightly and at but one point" and are likewise subject to transformation through time.[8] How can these 'acts of translation' in historical contexts be apprehended as continuous productions of meaning through contextual shifts? The volumes of this series are structured with reference to the discourses of travelling concepts of design and art education which, with always shifting connotations and attributions of meaning, keep the schools and initiatives in a process of constant exchange and motion. In the process, how do they resist the temptation of a concept of legacies that are linked with the Bauhaus tradition? By also bringing into view the divisions, the untranslatable, the faults that, as Doris Bachmann-Mehdick emphasises, place historical processes of change "in a tension-filled confrontation with contrasts and similitudes and, in doing so, bring into focus a fractured range of meanings through distortions of history".[9]

In this sense, travelling concepts rather describe 'routes of appropriation' that do not follow the notion of a chronological sequence of past, present, and future, but move between different geographies, times and cultures. Thus, this book seeks to map the 'bumpy route' of the reform of education as a pluriversal, supportive, reciprocal design practice that aspires to manifest as practical utopia in the web of asymmetric knowledge regimes, geopolitical structures, hegemonial institutional frameworks and imperial economies. In conversations, field notes, reports and historiographical essays, the blind spots of the modern design discourse come to light. Discontinued endeavours, departures, and distortions are reflected alongside alternative forms of collective design activism, giving a stage to the many diverse movements in search of emancipatory, supportive, pluriversal design activity in historic and contemporary transformation processes.

1   1   Singanapelli Balaram. *The Barefoot Designer. Design as Service to Rural People.* Ahmedabad, 1998. https://www.bauhaus-imaginista.org/files/The_Barefoot_Designer_S.Balaram.pdf?0bbf-55ceffc3073699d40c945ada9faf=63fc46c58d54e-4a4e3822f0436c65146 , accessed 7 June 2023.

2   Alison Clarke. 'Design for Development, ICSID and UNIDO. The anthropological turn in 1970s Design', in: *Journal of Design History*, vol. 29, no. 1, February 2016, pp. 43–57, here p. 46.

3   Ibid.

4   Tim Ingold. *The Perception of the Environment.* London: Routledge, 2000, p. 339.

5   Cited after Claudia Mareis and Nina Paim. 'Introduction. An Attempt to Imagine Design Otherwise', in: id. (eds.). *Design Struggles. Intersecting Histories, Pedagogies and Perspectives* (PLURAL). Amsterdam: Valiz, 2021. p. 16.

6   Arturo Escobar. 'Transiciones: A Space for Research and Design for Transitions to the Pluriverse', in: *Design Philosophy Papers*, no. 13, 2015, pp. 13–23, https://www.tandfonline.com/doi/full/10.1080/14487136.2015.1085690, accessed 7 June 2023.

7   See Mareis and Paim (as note 5), p. 20.

8   Walter Benjamin. *The Task of the Translator*, http://www.ricorso.net/rx/library/criticism/guest/Benjamin_W/Benjamin_W1.htm, accessed 22 April 2023.

9   Doris Bachmann-Medick, 'Übersetzung zwischen den Zeiten. Ein travelling concept?', in: *Saeculum, vol. 67, no.1, 2017*, p. 42.

Editorial by
JJ Adibrata, farid rakun (Gudskul);
Katja Klaus, Philipp Sack (Bauhaus Dessau Foundation)

Decolonising design education, decolonising education design

2

A word of warning: to talk about the title of this book collectively is an endeavor bound to fail, prone to a variety of misunderstandings, frictions and arguments. Each constituent calls for interpretation and nego-tiation—what we mean when we say 'decolonisation', 'design' and 'education' is by no means clear. Nei-ther is it clear what we mean when we say 'we'. So let's start with that. The fragmented subject trying to make sense of these terms consists of four indivi-duals affiliated to two very different cultural institu-tions operating in very different contexts: Gudskul (G) and the Academy of the Bauhaus Dessau Founda-tion (B). What follows is an attempt to account for the disparities of perspectives arising from these differ-ences, to make them productive rather than to temper them for the sake of some supposed universalism: a montage of fragments co-edited into a shared online document over the period of two weeks at the begin-ning of rainy season/autumn 2022.

G Gudskul, a Jakarta-based public learning space of collective study and contemporary art ecosystem, has been organising an annual collective study pro-gramme since 2018. The programme is conceived as a sharing platform intended to disseminate a sense of initiative in artistic and cultural endeavors in a society committed to collectivism. Gudskul sincerely believes in sharing and working together as two very vital elements in developing contemporary art, culture, and their ecosystems. The collectives in-volved in the study programme come from various contexts, united by the fact that they come from ex-colonies and see the need for infrastructures that are more supportive of the practice and development of art and design in the realm of discourse, production, presentation, appreciation, education and conservation. The practices initiated by these arts organisations or collectives are their way of taking on a role in developing these very infrastructures. They organise art projects as part of their contribution to society through various forms: workshops, sharing sessions, discussions, exhibitions, publications, etc.

B The Bauhaus Dessau Foundation, in turn, is not a learning space per se, but is tasked with preserving the legacy of one such institution. In the European history of culture, design, art and architecture of the twentieth century, the Bauhaus occupies a special role. As one of the first schools of design (Hochschule für Gestaltung), it faced the question of how to seize the dynamics of modernity with the means of design, operating when western industrial societies were going through a time of crisis. Even though the school was founded in the historical moment when Germany had to cede control of the places it had colonised to other European powers, the Bauhaus and the people affiliated to it benefited from and contributed to perpetuating colonial structures, both during the fourteen years of its operation and after its closure in 1933. As a hybrid institution situated at the intersection of different epistemologies and functional logics (that of an archive, a world heritage site, and a school), the

Bauhaus Dessau Foundation has been striving to rewrite the euro-centric history of art and design education for many years through the research and education programmes of its Academy department, focusing on transcultural dialogues and the global entanglements of western modernity.[1]

DECOLONISING DESIGN EDUCATION: LOOKING INWARDS, LOOKING BACK

B   As Regina Bittner has written in her preface, enforcing western educational systems onto the colonised communities was a key instrument of colonial rule. The establishment of educational institutions in their colonies modelled on European schools and universities served a dual purpose: colonial powers imposed particular western forms of knowledge on the colonies by claiming their universal validity, thereby marginalising and discrediting local epistemologies. They also employed these institutions in order to forge alliances with local elites willing to comply with (and/or administer) colonial rule in exchange for limited powers and privileges. Art and design schools played a crucial role in this project, as their curricula transposed the western canon of making and representing onto local traditions of cultural expression with the aim of training a cheap workforce for the manufacturing industries producing goods for the colonising powers. In spite of this initial mission however, it would be short-sighted to simply declare art and design schools mere instruments of exploitation. It were precisely these institutions that became hot-

2   How can we address existing colonial
structures with their blurred temporalities and
territorialities while at the same time
acknowledging our own complicity in them?

beds of anticolonial resistance and testing grounds
for a post-independence social order when countries in various regions of the Global South broke away
from colonial rule. Furthermore, they became agents
of postcolonial identity building as they contributed to
a revaluation of local crafting traditions and modes
of representation.

G   The long history of colonisation produces mixed
values resulting from the process of imitation, adjustment and equalisation of what is absorbed from colonialism, and from the exchange of information and
knowledge which further widens its horizons on the local values prevailing in it. To realise that educational,
social, art and cultural systems from the colonial her-

itage are a result of imitation and adjustment processes, means realising they are obsolete and no longer relevant to the vision, ideals and imagination of our contemporary contexts. The western education system, with its modernist perspective, tends to see everything through the lens of productivity and universality which is oriented towards a capitalist vision of human development. Looking at the context in which these initiatives are growing, it becomes obvious that they are in the midst of society with all its complex problems.

B   The obsolescence of colonial educational institutions then leads to the question of what could emerge from these ruins. We are thus exploring the practical conclusions contemporary western cultural institutions need to draw from their colonial complicity. What does decolonisation mean for the mission of a European world heritage site that is used to being considered relevant? How do we as an institution imbued with western tradition and privilege account for the manifold and often conflicting histories of anticolonial struggle, their contemporary effects and potential futures? How can we address existing colonial structures with their blurred temporalities and territorialities while at the same time acknowledging our own complicity in them? How can we, with the means at our disposal within our institutional boundaries, make a meaningful contribution to subverting these conditions?

B One strategy we are exploring with this project is the gesture of de-centring ourselves from the narrative we present. Instead of assuming the 'influence' and the Bauhaus as a 'centre' radiating out into a non-European 'periphery', we find it important to acknowledge the many interconnections that linked art and design schools throughout the world and throughout the twentieth century, and give room to alternative developments in design education. We are drawing from the manifold experiences and encounters that have emerged from previous projects conducted by the Bauhaus Dessau Foundation, such as *School Fundamental*, a festival on art and design education, the various editions of the research programme *Bauhaus Lab*, a series of hybrid conferences called *Bauhaus Study Rooms*, or the *Open Studios* programme for experimental teaching.[2] All of these projects fundamentally rely on practices of inviting and listening, as well as on de-linking art and design pedagogies from the modernist tradition. They have initiated continuous, mutual learning processes with a wide array of collaborators, thus opening up the historical narrative to include alternative models for collective agency. It is from this practice that the collaboration with Gudskul emerged. Since 2019, the Academy of the Bauhaus Dessau Foundation and Gudskul have engaged in a continuous dialogue spanning different educational formats and encounters, sometimes in person, oftentimes online. The reciprocal exposure to very different modes of instituting gave way to the realisation that rather than a shared set of references in academic decolonial discourse, a steadfast commitment to collaboration can be a route leading to subverting colonial legacies. Asking the right questions and drawing appropriate conclusions falls short of this challenge; the decisive step towards mutual liberation lies in putting these conclusions into practice. By committing to the principle of collaboration, we hope to steer clear of two major epistemic risks: on the one hand, turning this project into a narcissist exercise in introspection by only focusing on criticising our own privileges, on the other, exoticising decolonial discourses by deliberately not engaging in the conversation at all.

2

Learning does not only consist of cognitive acts, but also of physical actions. Understanding is gained not only in the heads of the actors, but also in their guts.

G These meeting points, made possible by continuous engagements between Bauhaus Dessau and Gudskul, represent attempts to converge stories from established histories and on-the-ground practices on equal footings—when theories meet stories. These acts create spaces where decolonisation is not only represented or talked about, but directly rehearsed in its messy, imperfect realities. Learning, therefore, does not only consist of cognitive acts, but also of physical actions. Understanding is gained not only in the heads of the actors, but also in their guts. The result, therefore, is porous, multi-directional, and constantly on-going.

2

BLURRING INSIDE AND OUTSIDE

B To come back to the introductory question, will we ever arrive at a set of clear-cut definitions for each of the three terms that make up the title of this issue? Probably not. Will this book convey a multiplicity of fleeting, competing, sometimes incommensurable perspectives on the meaning of decolonisation, design and education? We certainly hope so. The spectrum of contributions selected for this issue reflects the different modes of instituting that Gudskul and the Academy of the Bauhaus Dessau Foundation have subscribed to. The part commissioned by the Bauhaus consists of two historical case studies on schools that have emerged from decolonisation struggles, and two conversations about the discourses around decolonisation in the field of design studies in and beyond academic institutions situated in the former metropolises of the political geography of colonialism. These contributions are interwoven with in-depth reports about and reflections on education practices in formerly colonised regions, shared by ten art and design collectives based in Southeast and Central Asia as well as in Africa upon the invitation of Gudskul. By demonstrating how each collective seeks to activate local ways of seeing and doing both within and beyond existing institutional landscapes and colonial continuities, these contributions firmly ground the theoretical and historical explorations in empirical findings, providing valuable insights into the tactics and strategies employed in decolonial struggles, and into the way they are being related to what are conceived to be the benchmarks of decolonial discourse.

In her essay on the case studies submitted to the 1979 *Design for Development* conference, organised by the United Nations Industrial Development Organisation and the International Council of Societies of Industrial Design in Ahmedabad and Bombay (now Mumbai), Suchitra Balasubrahmanyan examines how design discourses and practices in post-independence India were largely animated by ideas revolving around the notion of modernisation. The desire to turn art and design schools into agents of change in decolonial struggles is echoed in Ola Uduku's contribution. Her article sheds light onto the meshwork of political alliances and international solidarity movements involved in the planning, construction and operation of learning spaces in

Africa, and explores both the potentials and perils of these endeavors in utopian place-making.

The epistemological implications of such decolonial practices as presented in both the historical studies and the reports shared by the ten art and design collectives are the subject of the contributions by <u>Nina Paim</u> and <u>Pedro Oliveira</u>, both reacting to a set of questions by Regina Bittner.

G With certain experiments that depart from the reality around them, specific contexts and localities, the organisations and art collectives invited to share their insights create various methods and models that are most appropriate to answer and respond to existing needs. Not infrequently, these methods and models are not something completely new, but a creative response to what is existing and happening in the community. When offered to the community, experimentation with these methods and models changes its form into horizontal learning processes.

These organisations and art collectives have grown and functioned as a receptacle that can continuously sustain the capacity to read, understand, and negotiate with the realities in their community, seeking its relevance and responding to its needs and positions within today's context. They become a motor, an agency that can adapt to or be inspired by their community and is able to read and respond to the rapid changes in society.

From an internal perspective, the art organisation or art collective space is often seen as a place for learning and experimenting for its members. Of the many organisations and artists who manage spaces like that, many do not come from an arts background but from all kinds of fields. This makes the space a hub where artistic and non-artistic ideas meet. For us, this is important because we believe that art and design require a way of looking from various points of view, from a variety of contexts. Working as art organisations and collectives, they often propose ideas related to social issues using various approaches through art and design to interact with the community, learn from them and offer new ideas based on the knowledge they gain from these interactions.

The knowledge about art and design they have experienced so far is the result of a process that they have learned, and learned to believe in, which comes from the West. Thus, what they think is good in principle is in practice the perception that they get from the knowledge that comes from the West. When organisations and art collectives rooted in a locality carry out their practice, they tend to see what is good according to the local perceptions, and often that is outside of what is generally agreed upon. The practice of working with local communities opens up many boundaries, goes beyond what so far has been accepted as 'standard' and finds other ways of learning.

The spaces run by art organisations and collectives are also imagined as safe places for people and ideas, where various perspectives meet and trans-

We are using this opportunity in a deeper understanding of time, the past as a thing to reflect
on in the present, in order to imagine what's next.

form into a new idea, finding its function and relevance. The nature of these spaces is also to be open
to the community. People can come in and learn from
each other, sustaining the ideas, imaginations, sensibilities, values, and visions, to define and distrib-
ute things that they consider as important knowledge.

In the spirit of sustaining one's practice, the
contributions made by the following collectives are
not specifically made for this book. We are using this
opportunity in a deeper understanding of time, the
past as a thing to reflect on in the present, in order to
imagine what's next.

ba-bau AIR, a collective based in Hanoi, presents
and reflects on their practices on running a shared
space. Through establishing a space, they experiment
with the possibilities of a mutual learning environ-

ment, understood here as a fleeting constellation of humans and the way they obtain ownership of a space both with regards to its physical and spiritual qualities. Appropriately relying on evidence that is explicitly anecdotal, babau AIR demonstrate that even the shared practice of doing nothing, of inhabiting a space, can help to spark unintentional learning processes. Pangrok Sulap, a printmaking collective from Sabah, explores ways of conducting a collaborative practice that is radical both in the sense of its political demands and in the sense of it being firmly rooted in the communities they work with. Their contribution highlights the methods of collaboration they employ: activities that allow participation from diverse communities, making full use of public and open spaces for shared events. The name of Manila-based Salikhain Kolektib stems from the collective's belief that art is a form of research, and that, in turn, research is also a creative process. 'Salikhain' comes from the Filipino words *sali, saliksik, likha,* and *malikhain* ('participate', 'research', 'create', and 'creative'). In this issue, Salikhain Kolektib reports and reflects on several programmes engaging with local communities, harnessing local knowledge in a broader aspect and creating participatory works through art and design practices. Drawing from methods such as participatory mapping, they seek to deconstruct the colonial imagination imposed on a given place by allowing members of the communities they work with to give shape to their on-the-ground perspective on controversial government policies.

In their contribution, BiSCA (Bishkek School of Contemporary Art) report on forming the *School of Methodology of Art Research* in 2021 to create a platform for sharing experiences in art practices and methodologies of art research as a process of decolonising knowledge and thinking. Through this prism, the members of BiSCA look back at some of the projects they conducted with state museums in Kyrgyzstan, and identify these sites as bearers of a dormant potential for cultural transformations which has a huge potential for the development of social relations. The following contribution shifts the focus to a different region: Another Roadmap Africa Cluster (ARAC) is a part of the *Another Roadmap School,* an international network of practitioners and researchers who are working to establish art education as an engaged practice in museums, cultural institutions, educational centres, and grassroots organisations in 22 cities on four continents. They develop methodologies as tools to revisit and challenge old theories, welcoming new evolving perspectives on learning in a collaborative process. Lineo Segoete of ARAC's Maseru working group sheds light on the practicalities of pan-African coordination. Asking "what if the ghosts of our troubled histories have no resting place?", she reflects on how collective observations and reflections on the colonial infrastructures conditioning ARAC's practice inform their theoretical work. Based in Jakarta, the UnconditionalDesign collective runs an online platform documenting and archiving unconditional interventions in mass-produced consumer

2   Besides addressing colonial legacies in its content (a theme), this book intends to put into practice one way to do things differently—namely, collectivity, a model Gudskul continuously puts forward, experiments with, and believes in (a method).

goods as a study of informal design practices and street innovation across Indonesia. This method of participatory documentation and archiving through Instagram has been quite successful. Over the past five years, they have been able to collect hundreds of case samples from all over the archipelago. Using their contribution as an opportunity to take stock of their archiving practice and the design research workshops they have hitherto conducted, Unconditional-Design propose to broaden the view to see and document similar phenomena in other cities in Southeast Asia or worldwide. Hong Kong-based Asia Art Archive (AAA) is a hybrid institution dedicated to the production and exchange of knowledge about artistic practices across the continent. Through these practices, they seek to stimulate a critical and artistic dialogue in society. The contribution by Asia Art Archive reports on several programmes initiated in the past few years, developing strategies and approaches for their education projects organised in several regions in Asia. Furthermore, the authors talk about how the concept 2 of 'Asia' as a generalising projection with origins in the West relates to their practice.

Load Na Dito, a collective based in Manila, sketches out the first edition of *Kabit at Sabit,* a 2019 exhibition held across the Philippine archipelago. Repurposing a pre-colonial local tradition to stage works of art in public, the project sought to create a shared space to reflect and reimagine society in the run-up to the general election. With the idea of holding future editions, Load Na Dito regard the exhibition as a learning process, an alternative form of school that enables salutary tensions between trial and error, theory and praxis. In a poetic dispatch from Bandung, Omnikolektif contemplate their practice by positioning themselves to (and distancing themselves from) the existing institutional landscape in the field of art education, especially with regards to the dominant and prestigious Institut Teknologi Bandung, established by the Dutch in early 1920s and thus considered to be one of the oldest higher education institutions in Indonesia. In this contribution, they are joined by historian Changkyu Lee, who researches alternative models of art distribution and thus provides additional context to their seemingly simple gesture of home-making. Serrum is a Jakarta-based art collective focusing on education. For this contribution, Serrum members summarise a discussion of PRESISI, a collaborative group consisting of education practitioners to share ideas around contextual educational practices which are a reflection of the post-colonial context in Indonesia. Looking back on the publicly funded PRESISI programme, they are exploring the question whether colonial continuities with regards to institutions are bound to entail such continuities with regards to methodologies and epistemologies in art and design education, or if (and how) they can be subverted.

This book, besides addressing colonial legacies in its content (a theme), intends to put into practice one way to do things differently: through collectivity, a model Gudskul continuously puts forward, experiments with, and believes in (a method). What readers are experiencing, consequently, is a snapshot or a cross-section of this ongoing journey, taking the Bauhaus Dessau as its slicer—an active conspirator in making a particular part of this peregrination public. This collective journey is made out of crossings of many paths going in different directions. These public instances, when we 'produce' something to be 'reaped' in order to 'nourish' ourselves as well as others, can be understood as 'harvests'. These harvests come in different formats. One such format is *Fridskul* (Fridericianum as a school) at documenta fifteen in Kassel, Germany, a large-scale contemporary art exhibition (which most of the collectives and initiatives were part of). Another format is the joint edition of a volume like this one—enabling reflection on the past in order to have a stake in the future. The collective journey has a life of its own. If it is strong, it can become independent from the individual and group that formed it. These harvests are opportunities to be generous, by sharing and trusting that seeds can be planted in others.

2

B We are publishing this book in a moment when postcolonial theories and practices are being confronted with what Walter Benjamin described as "a moment of danger".[3] Not only are communities in postcolonial societies facing the challenge of organising collective selfhood in the context of crisis-ridden late global capitalism after the utopian calls to national liberation have subsided. In Germany specifically, the emancipatory potential of postcolonial theory and the legitimacy of voices from the Global South have lately been subject to a wholesale condemnation by reactionary forces. Continuing the conversation is our way of positioning ourselves in these debates.

1   This is exemplified in the exchanges between the Bauhaus and Kala Bhavana, Santiniketan (see t1p.de/santiniketan), and between Hochschule für Gestaltung Ulm and the National Institute of Design in Ahmedabad (see t1p.de/ahmedabad).

2   See t1p.de/programmes

3   On the concept of history, VI.

Notes on running a space

3

To run a space, we must first make a space.

To make a space, we must find the right locale—or let the right locale find us.

Things happen at the right time and place—in the spirit of *Duyên*.[1]

In this context, 'running a space' means manifesting, thinking, making, working, inhabiting and loving that space.

ON SPACE

3   1 Space is a Body

Its 'flesh' holds its potential and possibilities. It breathes with agency and a sense of self; it is never to be exploited. As cohabitants, we interact with this 'body' everyday; sometimes we touch, sometimes we purposely do nothing.

2 Space is a repository, a vessel, a carrier bag. It holds the spirits, energies and emotions of those who encounter it. Like us, a space, too, needs to rest. The question is, can we calculate the amount of resting time a space needs? *Stage(s) of Resting (dual channel video, Kassel 2022) poses a question about "resting" to all our collective members. Nguyễn Duy Anh (filmmaker, member of the ba-bau AIR collective) created a video about our space in Hà Nội while pest control measures were being carried out. As with an intervention, with reverence, we tried not to be in that space, we tried not to touch it. During that moment, it was as if the space was resting. We learned that resting time is perhaps*

not meant to be scheduled, much as how a person only rests when they are sick. A space has its own preferences and logic for rest and it can be difficult to distinguish the space's physical and spiritual needs. More than once, spirits who have resided here for nearly a century have scolded us about how we treat the space. One time, our dead landlord reminded us about the importance of his beloved kitchen table by shutting off our electronic devices. There are unspoken boundaries that allow no errors. And if there are disagreements about these sacred lines, we are reminded of this from time to time by the space's observers.

3

What is sacredness anyway? How we revere a space is personal. Our collective is formed around a shared affection toward the space. But, at the same time, such reverence can be rendered irrelevant in the eyes of those who do not share our feelings. Therefore, these tensions or contradictions yield a constant process of negotiation between the differing observers and caretakers.

3 Space is never fixed.

Space fluctuates, expands and contracts. Its ownership is fluid. It has 'AIR', attitude and volatility. Anything and everything inside and outside a space can and should leave even more space in flux. One cannot own the space, but one might claim ownership of it and further nourish the space in close conjunction with non-ownership itself.

4 Space is unreal. Space is fictional.
The house is unreal. The house is fictional.
Our inhabitation is real. Our being is real.
We create the space.
We create the house.
We are the space.
We are the house.

5 Adapt as situations arise. Challenge the norms
3   that may grow out of such situations.

ON OWNERSHIP

6 A co-owned space is where each and every oc-
cupant shares the responsibility of owning it.
A space can run by itself without a specific
owner because everyone is both owner and non-
owner.

There is no distinction between hosts and guests.
To share domesticity, to share even the most
mundane task like cleaning the house or water-
ing the plant, means to give permission to the
new occupants to join in and take charge of their
newfound ownership. Sharing the sense of
ownership is as simple as having the key available to anyone at any time, helping to wash
dishes or rearrange bookshelves. Those who use
the space have equal access to it. The space
is to provide comfort and to be used at will, whether for working, resting, or avoiding traffic jams.
The space only asks that those who use it main-

tain its condition so that other people can feel at home too.

Naturally, the space is in a state of flux, like the waves on a riverbed. It is transparent, resilient, and moves at its own pace.

7 A safe space is where everyone is free to keep to their own speed and pace, without being submitted to stress or any outer forces (the position of the sun, for example).

There is no such thing as a universal sense of time.

3

Time is relative. Time stays still, ceases to exist or is neglected in this designated setting—or seems to be.

Time is shared and cannot be owned.

Here, there is no fixed temporality.

In the space at 82A Thợ Nhuộm, bà bầu Hà Nội, time bends according to the density, energy and narrative of whatever is happening. The first year of the pandemic entered straight into an oblivion outside our timeline: contactless, eventless, tasteless. During the summer of the second pandemic year, two days after the public emergency announcement, our residency turned into a quarantine shelter and stayed that way for two eternal months. Usually after dinner, surprise gatherings happen. Several teapots worth of dialogue pass by. Either someone will ruefully take leave because our neighborly bike watchman cannot stay up any later, or someone will rush to the shop to buy a toothbrush so that they can stay the night. During a kitchen talk, each revels in their own orbit: Linh gave our guest speaker cô Síu a surprise haircut, Nga washed the dishes, Chung swept the floor, other attendees prepared watermelon and record-ed the session. All at once, in the same room, unscripted, forceless, well-woven and conflict-free.

8 Look after the house, the cats, the plants and the neighbour(hood), both voluntarily and obligatorily, in order to safeguard a robust and healthy future for the community. A collective is not only about a particular group of people; it is also about its surrounding life and milieu. Everything which nurtures and plants seeds can further the growth of the collective and its prac-tice.

ON THE DESIGN AND USAGE OF THINGS

9 Use the least materials in designing the space and reuse and recycle whenever possible. Avoid hoarding! Assign purpose and potentiali-ties to every object within the space. Objects that lack these should be given to those in need.

10 Anything can be mobile, replaceable, easy to dismantle and reassemble, both in form and in function. Depending on the purpose, all users have all rights and responsibilities towards the space and the things inside it at all times.

ON LEARNING

11 Occupants are encouraged to utilise, design, and facilitate the space according to their own practice and interests.

TWO APPROPRIATIONS; TWO LESSONS

Nghia's reading sessions can go by without anyone saying a word. Some Sundays can pass quietly under the thick summer air that hangs heavy before the rain. Between the words and between the pages, a dense atmosphere pushes down on ba-bau

3

Duy Anh & Nga's cinema Hoa Quỳnh (epiphyllum flower) airs from eight in the evening to three in the morning (according to the circadian rhythm of two sleepless cinema enthusiasts). Seemingly out of thin air and out of a non-existent budget, they put up a theater-grade movie screen. Twice a week, they feast on films, sometimes with a drink, sometimes with guests, sometimes neither, but always with laughter. Shortly after, nobody knows how, Nga is admitted to the University of Theater and Performing Arts of Hanoi.

Such appropriations stretch, push, and teach. Thus, the people learn. The space also learns.

1 *Duyên* (English: destined encounter, serendipity/ Chinese: 緣 yuán) **is a noun, a verb, an adjective, a feeling, a spell, a sound, a space.** *Duyên* **is a character, a sign, a moment, a fantasy, etc.**

Empowering community through art

Instead of being limited to traditional art institutions or galleries, we create a method of collaboration in the form of activities that allow participation from diverse communities, making full use of public and open spaces for community events. The more relaxed you are, the better. As a result, we emphasize the egalitarian and democratic principles that strive to destroy the notion that society can only enjoy art as an observer or that it must be instructed to do so.

On the other hand, we believe that collaboration should be organically self-organised by the collaborators rather than having a leader who gives instructions. Anyone has the right to speak up if something needs to be corrected. Individualism is rejected in favor of collaboration, which encourages all parties to participate. We do not reject mistakes because, as humans, we must accept and be open to all situations. We cannot rely solely on one person to make decisions because, in collective life, the system of collaboration must have a mutual agreement at its heart. In our experience, when an individual decision is required, it should benefit the entire project rather than the individual. Mutual discussion can improve an idea, and this is a process that will always occur between collaborators. This ongoing dialogue is what will foster trust.

Playing the guitar and singing songs in a local language that the public is familiar with is the most efficient way for us to socialise in the community. This process enables us to identify individuals who have a vibrant spirit, are eager to socialise and enjoyable

4

to meet. As visitors to a community, it is our responsibility to put aside our egos and to initiate contact. As a result, there is a recognition that collaboration should seek not to assimilate, degrade or transform collaborators into a homogeneous or static entity but rather to explore their latent abilities. Finally, family relationships and friendships are successfully formed as a result of various levels of social interaction such as this, thereby breaking down the relationship system between, for example, employees and employers.

The relationship between us and other collaborators is not limited to a single project using this method. However, it will help to establish a network in other locations and provide opportunities for future projects. We were able to foster a consensus among new contacts and sometimes bring old friends together to make a project. In Kota Kinabalu, for example, we collaborated with several local artists to create a community space. There is a record store run by a friend from the music scene as well as a café run by the collective Borneo Komrad. There are also bookstores, crafts and clothing stores. We take our inspiration from Gudskul Indonesia, which has successfully created an ecosystem for several collectives to come together under one larger roof. For us, this marks the start of a long-term collaboration between several local collectives. And our collective system adapts to new collaborators, adding elements such as transparent discussions.

We believe that the true goal of collaboration is found because each of us is an artist with a different and unique level of creativity. Future collaborations will produce results that are not based on object-based absolutes, a reaction to a notion of contemporary art that overinflates the art market and institutions. A collaboration based on continuous engagement, a mix of different individuals who are open to shaping themselves in the interests of mutual progress, will create and promote democracy by bringing art to a society that is not used to it. Indeed, many people believe that art should only be owned by those who are talented, such as those who are good at drawing. No. We consider aesthetics to be secondary. For example, the majority of our posters or artworks make use of popular local terms. This is because we believe that by using vernacular languag-

4

Playing the guitar and singing songs in a local language that the public is familiar with is the most efficient way for us to socialise in the community.

es, or those commonly used by locals, we will be able to share ownership with the community. We are always involved in every local event and collaborate with community organisations of various disciplines through our collective practice. This enables us to reach a broader range of audiences, not just those associated with the arts.

We express ourselves through the art of wood carving prints. We also provide the same service to the community. We oppose any action that has the potential to harm society and the environment. This is because the majority of today's local collaboration systems are already influenced by those with vested interests when the capitalist system emerges. This system has a direct impact on the indigenous peoples around us and pollutes the existing traditional system. Traditional economic activities, for example, are increasingly being forgotten due to their incompatibility with modern life. We encourage the community around us, with a small effort, to maintain simple lifestyle practices in order to restructure problems that arise and fight for their survival. Comprehensive community participation enables the formation of stronger defenses in the face of current unfavorable and oppressive developments.

This aligns with our slogan, "Jangan Beli, Bikin Sendiri" (Don't buy it, do it yourself). The tradition of creative and alternative solutions that do not rely on external elements—for example, communal work between rural communities to build houses, natural resources that are available in a community that they use sustainably without completely damaging the ecosystem—has become one of the traditions passed down from generation to generation. Capitalist elements, such as logging, have an impact on and pollute the local ecosystem. According to our observations, all of the local community collaborations in which we participate already exhibit these characteristics. In fact, things like this teach us a lot about preserving a place's traditions, culture and history through an artistic approach.

We not only produce woodcut print with the community, but we are also involved in village activities throughout our involvement. In addition to documenting history and oral traditions, such as the craft house project in Kampung Keiyep, Ranau, we also had the opportunity to learn farming, hunting and even medicine from the villagers. We believe in the 'teaching and learning' process because we believe that everyone is a teacher. Each of us has a unique set of skills. We cannot be arrogant because of the few advantages we have, because the village people are very knowledgeable. Thanks to this symbiotic factor, we can learn a lot from how they solve problems with the resources they have. Being aware of this, we do not consider ourselves to be artists who bring art to the public. Rather, it is merely a medium or communication space for us to connect with the community.

We strive to create works that have a social impact. We believe that art can be a very effective medium of communication in developing societies.

For us, art is an effective medium connecting the collective and society. As a result, we produce a large number of graphic works in the form of messages and criticism that cover a wide range of topics, including human rights issues, politics, tradition, culture and environmental topics. Building networks with different layers of society is also critical for us to understand every issue and problem that arises in our community.

4

Decolonising art, research and education through participatory, interdisciplinary practices

5

'Salikhain' comes from the Filipino words *sali, saliksik, likha* and *malikhain* ('participate', 'research', 'create' and 'creative'.) The name is a manifestation of the collective's belief that art is a form of research, and that, in turn, research is also a creative process. A collective composed of artists, researchers, environmental scientists, community workers and educators, the name Salikhain articulates our inquiry to localise and decolonise our different practices. We desire to access the wisdom of the antidisciplinary, the social, the relational and even the spiritual. These qualities inform our working principles: a commitment to transdisciplinarity, using participatory methods, and leveraging art's potential to raise social capital, to communicate, and lobby policies for local communities.

Shared below are some of our activities and projects showing these principles in action.

SALI: PARTICIPATION
5 ## DECENTRALISING AND REORGANISING
HIERARCHIES OF KNOWLEDGE [1]

PARTICIPATORY MAPPING
Participatory Three-Dimensional Modelling (P3DM) was developed in the 1980s by scientists, geographers and community workers as a method for building 3D maps with communities. In 2007, this mapping method was applied for disaster risk reduction and management (DRRM) planning by the Philippine Geographical Society.

Community-centred approach: Participatory mapping facilitators guide participants in making an accurate 3D model of a certain place. The method employs a community-centred approach wherein the participants are involved in deciding several aspects of both the mapping process and the output. Through the process of building the 3D map, participants can also improve their spatial awareness.

Exploring new materials—from styrofoam to wood: However, these 3D maps are typically made from styrofoam, rubber foam, or cardboard. Artist and woodworker Ralph Lumbres (Salikhain Kolektib) devised a method of participatory 3D modeling that uses plywood and sawdust. The resulting wooden maps are sturdier, eco-friendly, and have increased aesthetic value. The maps produced through the P3DM process devised and facilitated by Ralph Lumbres in Dingalan, Aurora (Philippines); Sulu-an Island, Guiuan (Philippines); and Hadiwarno, Pacitan (Indonesia), are the only documented P3DM maps that are made of wood.

SALIKSIK: RESEARCH
HARNESSING LOCAL KNOWLEDGE TO LOBBY
FOR POLICY CHANGE [2]

INCLUSIVE RESEARCH THROUGH
PHOTOGRAPHY

Photovoice is a participatory research method that places cameras in the hands of people in a community to capture and document their observations, perceptions, and even emotions. It was first introduced as 'photo novella' by Caroline Wang and Mary Ann Burris in 1994 to study public health-related issues. In this method, the photos serve as a starting point for conversation, generating a forum for communities to reach policy makers and lobby for change.

Using Photovoice for integrated risk management: In the Philippines, environmental researcher Juan Miguel Torres (Salikhain Kolektib) adapted Photovoice as a research method for *barangay* (village) disaster risk reduction and management planning. Torres' workshop design empowers community members to collect, process and analyse in-depth information on the capacities and vulnerabilities of their village. The approach inspires meaningful reflection on the community's strengths and weaknesses and the collected data are then used as a supplemental document for DRRM planning.

A spotlight on small island communities: Over 7,600 islands make up the nation-archipelago of the Philippines, most of which are categorised as small islands. Due to their remoteness and geographic separation from political and economic centres, these small island communities are typically the most at risk against escalating climate hazards. One output of the Photovoice workshops in Suluan and Homonhon Islands in Guiuan, Samar, is the successful documentation of the knowledge and good practices specific to small island communities— where people have had to rely on specific local skills, knowledge of their own environment, and exist-

56

ing mechanisms to survive and adapt to harsh climate conditions. Practices from these small islands may serve as models for education about disaster risk reduction in relation to managing the natural environment for larger communities as well.

Inclusive planning for persons with disabilities: Photovoice was also one of the methods used in the project *Lahat Dapat: Toolkit for inclusive DRRM planning*. The project addresses the disproportionate number of deaths and injuries among persons with disabilities during disasters. The toolkit includes innovative and creative ways of engaging persons with disabilities in DRRM planning, ensuring that response actions of the government are aligned to their actual needs.

LIKHA: CREATION/MALIKHAIN: CREATIVE RECLAIMING ART AS A PRACTICE IN EVERYDAY LIFE; AS AN EXPRESSION AND ARTICULATION OF LOCAL CONTEXTS [3]

5

SCULPTURES OF LOCAL BIODIVERSITY

In the participatory mapping project, Salikhain introduces the participants to the 3D modelling process through experiential learning. Before working on the 3D map itself, participants first learn basic sculptural techniques and woodworking by making relief sculptures.

Aside from being a pedagogical approach to teaching 3D modelling, the participants get to create art objects that they can keep and take home. In

Sulu-an, their sculptures also become a means to express and reflect their local culture, biodiversity and wildlife. The workshop also empowers women as they learn carpentry and how to use power tools. Some women made even more sculptures to create decorations for the village kindergarten.

IMAGES OF LIFE IN THE ISLANDS

Some of the project participants in the participatory photography project in Sulu-an Island, Guiuan, Eastern Samar, were fisherfolk, local village workers, market vendors, housewives and teachers. They were given a few weeks to a month to photograph the capacities and vulnerabilities of their villages using a disposable camera. The resulting images centre the perspective from within, offering a contrast to the tourists' gaze.

1   Projects: *Ligtas PAD*, Dingalan, Philippines, 2017; *Art for Resilient Communities*, Dingalan and Sulu-an Island, Philippines; Hadiwarno, Indonesia; Ubon Ratchathani, Thailand, 2019.

2   Projects: *Island Film Project*, Sulu-an Island and Homonhon Island, Philippines, 2017; *Art for Resilient Communities*, Dingalan and Sulu-an Island, Philippines; Hadiwarno, Indonesia; Ubon Ratchathani, Thailand, 2019; *Lahat Dapat: Toolkit for Inclusive DRRM*, Pasig City, Philippines, 2021–2022.

3   Projects: *Art for Resilient Communities*, Dingalan and Sulu-an Island, Philippines; Hadiwarno, Indonesia; Ubon Ratchathani, Thailand, 2019; *Disaster and Design* (exhibition), Tokyo Metropolitan Art Museum, Japan, 2019.

Decolonising the methodology of working with state museums

6

A conversation between Bermet Borubaeva, Oksana Kapishnikova, Alima Tokmergenova and Diana Ukhina on the past and the prospects of the Bishkek School of Contemporary Art (BiSCA).

BERMET BORUBAEVA What is the 'colonised' production of knowledge today? One can argue about definitions for a long time, but for me, the important understanding is that it is the alienation from context, from creation of meanings and their replacement with external cultural dominants. At the same time, the decolonisation of knowledge production is often a very traumatic process, but it is mostly the emancipatory experience of finding yourself, your context, your history, your background, your discourse and constituting it publicly. Using our platforms, we are running processes of decolonising knowledge and thinking.

In 2021, the *School of Methodology of Art Research* was launched by BiSCA in collaboration with Synergy art studio. Within the public educational programme, the curatorial team (Diana Ukhina, Bermet Borubaeva) has created a platform for sharing experiences in art practices and methodologies of art research. We, as participants/facilitators of BiSCA and Synergy together with other invited actors presented and analysed our own methodologies of art research.

For us, a methodology is the basis of creativity, it is a tool not only for scientists, but also for cultural workers. The important thing for us was that the School of Methodology of Art Research is built on self-organisation and solidarity, without any budgets, and with only personal inputs and resources. There is no hierarchy of knowledge, no teachers, there are equal participants in the process of information exchange. Shifting the focus of study to ourselves to our personal art practices became one of our active tools to decolonise knowledge in the context of artistic processes in Bishkek and to reflect this experience to the outside. Through the prism of the School of Methodology of Art Research, we shall now look at our work with state museums in Kyrgyzstan.

DIANA UKHINA Museums have a huge potential for the development of social relations and the formation of a space of reflectivity, search, inexplicable sensory experience and through this the harmonisation of social relations. In their potential, they can be as open as possible to everyone, without exception, on the basis of conditional separating identities, such as nationality, religion, gender, etc. Most of Kyrgyzstan's museums exist as an infrastructure filled with artifacts —interesting, valuable, containing power— but in a lifeless environment of silence and stillness. These spaces, mostly created during the Soviet period, are in no way centres of social life for local communities. They are storage facilities, some are in tolerable conditions, some are completely deplorable—empty, dusty, falling apart physically and mentally. The only exceptions are those museums whose agenda is in one way or another close to state values—patriarchal and nation-centric.

Over the past two years I have been working with the Gapar Aitiyev National Museum of Fine Arts, focusing on women's work. Our museum, like most museums in the world, tells a male-centred art history and broadcasts these views in its visual culture. Less than 5% of the main exposition shows works by female artists, the origins of which can always be reflected through gender display.

In 2020, I initiated *Art history of Kyrgyzstan of the 20th century in the practices of female artists* —a research diving into art history through their works and stories of the Soviet period: painting, graphics, sculpture and ceramics. My colleague Alima Tokmergenova and I are doing research as cultural actors who create their history, contemporaneity and memory from ourselves, and not from external dominant stories, canons and structures. We do a study of the museum's institutional memory about female artists, whose works are represented in the collection from its inception (1935) until the early 1990s, but for the most part are not available to the audience.

The museum's management was open to us as external independent researchers to:

1. carry out work with the museum library (sorting books, exhibition catalogues: identifying information about artists, their names, stories and getting to know the museum library memory);
2. create an online research exhibition of female artists from library materials;

3   work with the museum collection and make a curatorial exhibition from its closed funds; (exhibited about 140 works by 22 female artists)

4   cooperate with the museum to publish a catalogue about female artists based on the work done.

This openness of the museum's leadership allowed us to generate a long-term research base about female artists and start bringing impulses from our inside work as external actors.

However, the museum largely functions within the collapsing Soviet inertia—a good collection is basically from the last century; art forms are represented by painting, sculpture, graphics, folk arts and crafts; the museum understands itself, first and foremost, as a state institution, not a social one. There are many current problems: no permanent public programme; almost no scientific work; few staff members with relevant education; budget, covering only small salaries and utility costs.

It feels like museums work on separate islands on which life takes place, but on the whole, stagnation and loss are felt. This is a living creature in some aspects, but still more a sleeping creature. A creature on the basis of which it is possible to make cultural transformations of the whole country, if this force is awakened and connected with the dormant potentials of the museum network throughout the country.[1]

ALIMA TOKMERGENOVA Bishkek has several memorial museums dedicated to the life and work of artists and cultural figures. One of them is the house of the sculptor Olga Manuilova. Whenever we approach the administration of the museum, we see that they are always open to our suggestions and ideas, they are ready to collaborate. But when it comes to implementing our ideas, we understand that their work is primarily aimed at conserving the place, the history of the house. In 2015, we had the opportunity (based on our interest and conversations with the museum's leadership) to work with the collection of the Olga Manuilova Museum to create a two-week research exhibition titled *Art and emancipation: Olga Manuilova and her contemporaries*. Visitors got

I would like to expand this educational circle, opening spaces for audiences, visitors who can become accomplices, co-authors of the development process of a museum or cultural institution.

the opportunity to interact with the house-museum and its different parts in a different way. The budget for the research exhibition was less than 100 USD from our own resources.

Such days and work processes are very inspiring. We want to implement even more ideas in the museum, to make it a livelier space, so that visitors can come not only to see the exhibition, but to interact with it in various formats. And the artistic processes that can take place here should concern not only the past, but also the present, the moment in which we live, what we face today in culture and art as cultural actors and as spectators.

Based on this and not only this experience, we came to the Issyk-Kul region, initiating the *Participatory Museum* project for museum workers. There were three of us: art historian Oksana Kapishnikova, curator and researcher Diana Ukhina, and researcher Alima Tokmergenova. And it felt strange: what can we teach people who have been working in museums for almost all their lives? But perhaps this is where the problem is hiding. The museums of the Issyk-Kul region are located in a historical area that is developed for tourism, but the display and work experience are fundamentally built on what was created in the Soviet time.

The country does not train new museum specialists (in 2022 the faculty of art history was launched again after a long break). They are hired from sometimes vaguely related specialties, and everything rests on the older generation. And in the emerging economic conditions of the state, when culture and museums are funded on a residual basis, there are new challenges in working with the museum audience, and they require new approaches.

For three days on the shore of Issyk-Kul, we shared our experience, and the museum staff talked about their work, museums and the issues that concern them today. We talked about how to do audience research, art research, and how to create exhibitions on a small budget. The seminar was attended by employees of the local history museums of Cholpon-Ata, Balykchy, as well as the Centre for Nomadic Civilisation.

The Participatory Museum is an educational programme for employees of museums in the Issyk-Kul region, consisting of two parts: theoretical (a three-day seminar) and practical (research, creation of an exhibition and publication). The goal is to get acquainted with new museum practices. In the following months, participants of this project conducted audience research and artistic research, and we kept in touch with them, consulting and helping. The project assumed a small honorarium and a budget for research and display. And finally, in January 2022, two exhibitions opened.

The Issyk-Kul State Historical and Cultural Museum-Reserve of Cholpon-Ata presented the results of a research project on the history of the city, or rather Sovetskaya Street, which is the main street of the city. They displayed stories around it, based on archival data and oral histories of residents and eyewitnesses of different times. The Centre of Nomadic Civilisation in the village of Chon Sary Oi worked with communities. At the exhibition they presented a large display about the flora and fauna of the village, using interactive and multimedia.

As a result of the project, we created a zine-guide for the Participatory Museum, which included the working materials of the educational programme, intermediate stages of research, as well as photographs of the exhibitions. We believe that this zine can be used by other museum workers in different cities around the country.

Such communication with museums allows us to be together in the field of mutual learning. We learn from them, they take something from our experience, and we believe that they implement it into their practices. And I would like to expand this educational circle, opening spaces for audiences, visitors who can become accomplices, co-authors of the development process of a museum or cultural institution. They can become important cultural centres, public places of various levels, dedicated to the dissemination of knowledge, the exchange of experiences, as well as a space for experimentation and freedom.

OKSANA KAPISHNIKOVA The field of my interest is primarily small museums in Kyrgyzstan, which were formed not by a directive from the above/government, but by a grassroots initiative: self-organised cultural institutions, the so-called 'public museums'. And here the 'public' is not in its publicity but in the involvement of the community in the formation and functioning of the museum. What were the reasons for their occurrence, for whom did they work, what was their functionality, and how are they being run now?

In the 1960s and 1970s, there was a museum boom throughout the Soviet Union, including Kyrgyzstan. Everywhere in cities, villages and schools, 'public museums' were opened, forming a museum network. For the most part, these were historical-memorial and local history museums created for the purpose of archiving history and artifacts, educational activities, and representing mainly the interests of local communities.

These small museums constantly conducted active educational work with local communities, villagers or pupils who were direct participants in their formation and functioning. Today, the situation has changed radically. On the one side, this was due to museum inertia, low qualifications and low salaries of museum employees. And on the other side, there is no interest of the community, not only in development, but even in their support and visiting, and this is dictated by the fact that a museum does not change and nothing happens in it.

I want to know why museums are lifeless and little visited today. I understand which role the personal factor can play, if there is a desire to do something, create and change. Small museums based on the principle of self-organisation of a community or an individual are actively functioning, being filled and developed by its creators. Often, with the departure

By unlocking the potential of museums as possibly inclusive public structures, we can work with consciousness, free the collective imagination from dogmas regarding social order, remove social prohibitions on the mutual right to be ourselves and accept the boundaries of others.

of the ideologist of the museum, the process of stagnation or even regression begins in the institution.

At our local museum conferences, you can hear discussions on the topic of 'museum inertia' and how to overcome it. Alienation of labor is inherent in many state structures. In many cases this is due to the underestimation of knowledgeable workers, who have low salaries (30 to 45 EUR a month), which forces them to engage in additional earnings. They direct all their forces to survive, and not to create/ produce. Hence the alienation and inertia of labor. This situation leads to a certain vicious circle, which contributes to the closure of small museums.

The museum structure is primarily created, maintained and developed in the interests of the museum staff and the local community around which it is formed. Today, in the capitalist paradigm, the private begins to prevail over the public, when on the contrary, the development of the museum requires the predominance of public consciousness and creation. In collective co-creation, constant dialogue (viewer-museum), procedural understanding of the common cause, can be formed into something more.

DIANA UKHINA Thus, the methodological approaches of the BiSCA's work with institutional structures and the decolonisation of knowledge can be systematised as follows:

1   Study of the conditions of museums (content, infrastructure, relevance, openness, inertia)—focusing both museums in the regions (Museum of Participation project in Issyk-Kul and the Herzen Museum in the Talas region) and in the capital (KNMofFA named after G. Aitiev).

2   Work with museum collections, museum literature, implementation and promotion of curatorial and research approaches (KNMofFA named after G. Aitiev and the Herzen Museum in the Talas region).

3   Conducting educational programmes for museum employees about artistic methods of research, working with the audience, and transformation of museum from repository to social form (Museum of Participation)

All this can be described as 'education in practice' through the flow around solid structures. This is our conscious and unconscious agenda and the way to decolonise the artistic sphere, art education and ourselves from the rigid and patriarchal governmental structures. Only in this way, in our context, can an independent museum agenda be implemented, aimed at unlocking the potential of the museums and forming a harmonious social structure both between people and between humanity and the planet.

6

If we speak through the optics of the sociology of culture, culture determines social relations and superstructures. Thus, through the potential of museums as possibly inclusive public structures, we can work with consciousness, free the collective imagination from dogmas regarding social order, and remove social prohibitions on the mutual right to be ourselves and accept the boundaries of others.

Why are we?

7

The stance of the Another Roadmap Africa Cluster (ARAC)—and by extension that of Another Roadmap School—is that international policies on art education lack substantial, nuanced research on art education practices and epistemology in the varying socio-political contexts represented across Africa. We recognise that there exists insufficient critical engagement with the history and persistent hegemony of western concepts of art and education within the continent.

The starting point of our work: country, environment and discipline all inform what we end up contributing to the collective. This is to say, we are inspired and motivated by our societies and their politics, the spaces we occupy and the architecture and natural topography thereof, things both tangible and intangible and, of course, the conversations we participate in, listen to, and even overhear. Over the years, we have paid attention to our communication styles, to stress relief and self-care rituals, to how we eat and have fun. Our meetings therefore serve as melting pots for birth and rebirth. New processes and symbolic expressions emerge, culminating in practical approaches that reflect our various backgrounds.

OUR DESIGN FRAMEWORK

1 Exhibition kit
An open-ended method of art-making and learning in new company including:
█████ works developed through ARAC's collective methods;

◼◼◼ works emerging from ARAC members, own
practices;

◼◼◼ objects coming from artists associated with ARAC.
This tool is aimed primarily at members of ARAC
as they move around and represent the collective in
different contexts.

7   2◼◼◼ (Un)Chrono/Logical timeline
The timeline aims to locate histories of arts education
including the routing of personal narratives, firstly
in an African context and then abroad. The Johannesburg working group came up with this concept as a
way of coping with their struggle with the term 'history'.
In IsiZulu there is no HIStory, no masculine or fem-
inine, but rather the word *mlando*, which is also used
to define a stem of a plant or a story.

This stem-story represents time, the beginning
or the core essence of the story. This timeline, in
its (un)chronological nature, speaks to mlando beyond
the written, into the imagined, vocal, sonic and visual. Each iteration has different interactions calling
for a response and, in some instances, observation
and intergenerational engagement.

The timeline has had many public iterations and
manifests in a variety of ways. However, the format
is always the same. People grab a piece of paper and
share a significant historical moment in art, in history,
or in their own personal lives. These stories are spread
out in non-linear order on a plastic sheet or floor.
Afterwards, participants are invited to engage in the
story-telling and then share their impressions.

77

3 Travelling printing kit in a suitcase

This is a concept derived from the Medu Art Ensemble. The collective consisted of a group of cultural workers who would create posters as part of a protest art movement during the apartheid era, until their operation was brought to a violent end by the South African Defence Force in Gaborone, Botswana, in 1985. ARAC re-imagines this suitcase in the present. It consists of monoprint materials which can be used and adapted in any context. Medu searched for methods of producing graphics that used materials and skills that could be made available in community organisations and townships. Silkscreening could be developed as a relatively low-cost and available technology. Medu explored ways to adopt newer silkscreen technologies (such as photo stencil) to township conditions, where people might not have running water or electricity. By 1984, the graphics unit proposed producing and distributing the 'silkscreen workshop in a suitcase'. This would be a portable box (50 × 75 × 15 cm) with a silkscreen press that could print A2 posters, ink, squeegee and stencil material. This would enable township organisations to make posters even under ill-equipped or illegal conditions.

4 Radio play/archive activations

The nature of our mutual curiosity inevitably leads to the archive. We dig through this for audio-visual, photographic, aural and textual portals into the past to help us understand ourselves and our broader present social circumstances. One modality that has piqued our interest is radio and the performativity of it. Through radio plays we imagine scenarios in which we are privileged to hold conversations with our intellectual ancestors and ask them questions, whether hypothetical or philosophical.

5 Letter writing

7 One of the most important material symbols of solidarity is a letter. The Medu Art Ensemble newsletters contained letters. Their forms ranged from the ubiquitous standard 'letter to the editor' such as 'Letter from South Africa' (vol. 5, no. 2) to 'Poems from Vietnam' (vol. 3, no. 3). Indeed, these two examples may provide us with an entry into the significance of the letter over time. The letter as a means of communication is also a tool to mobilise.

6 Postcard method

Through this method originating in Lubumbashi, working groups leave each other messages that serve as either clues or highlights based on activities that occurred during absences. The messages can be statements, questions, phrases or tips through which members both maintain connections and feed into the knowledge economy we are cultivating.

7 Language workshops

Emma (Kampala working group) put it best when she said, "Indigenous African languages are regularly marginalised in law, in government, in journalism and in the education system within the very regions from which they originate. They are too rarely taken seriously by those with power as tools for serious discussion and debate. So-called intelligent people converse in the languages of former colonisers. Immigrants settling in Africa from Europe and North America and their descendants can prosper there for generations without ever needing to acquire a proficient grasp of the languages of the people among whom they live. The obverse is decidedly untrue."

As a response, members of the Lagos, Maseru, Joburg and Kinshasa working groups have each designed workshops around language. The Lagos working group through new interpretations of old writing systems, the Maseru working group through word invention and studies in orthography, the Joburg working group through the investigation of creolisation/pidginisation with Tsotsitaal (a mashup of Sesotho, IsiZulu, Afrikaans and English born in popular shebeens, taverns, restaurants, weddings, funerals or any social event) as the primary subject of study, and the Kinshasa working group through neologisms that have emerged within contemporary arts practice in DR Congo.

The erasure and dilution of native languages in Africa is propagated by the fact that people simply do not recognise the value in them from being conditioned to assume that colonial languages are superior. Through our interventions, we hope to transfer power back to the locality and even elevate the status of already existing languages by highlighting the value of the heritage and history embedded within them.

8 People who think together dance together

Based on the realisation that we are not meant to just meet and have presentations of research, feedback sessions and sessions to plan how to take our works back to our communities and constituencies, we made it a tradition to also dance together as a radical and emancipatory approach to culture, education and knowledge in post-independence Africa, the by-products of which are fun and stress relief.

9 Ecole du soir

The night school features a series of film screenings inspired by writer and director Ousmane Sembène. It is a pedagogical experiment animated through a deliberate screening of films that resonate with our practices as well as the questions we ask. We recognise that film is a powerful educational tool which can yield massive social transformation and disseminate information in a manner that also brings people together to engage in conversation. It puts the agency back into the community by showing them that they also have the capacity to tell their own stories.

10 The kitchen is a dancefloor

Virtually all the ARAC members enjoy cooking. It has therefore become a core part of our practice to exchange tastes and recipes from our various walks of life. As we cook, we discuss the different ways in which we nourish our bodies, approach cooking as a therapeutic practice, and practice care.

11 Walking, harvesting and publishing

As the title suggests, we walk as a means to help us process what we have just learned, heard, had communicated to us, and observed. The communication between bodies in motion and the mental bones at work play a big role in helping us harvest and process pieces of information until we reach

7   a point of understanding and internalisation. The next step, naturally, is publication.

WHAT ARE SOME OF THE QUESTIONS THAT LEAD US TO THESE METHODOLOGIES?

Now that Christianity has become 'African', where to bury the African ghosts?

What if the ghosts of our troubled histories have no resting place?

Are the artists who have been 'discovered' in harmony with the whole of their ecosystem?

How do we inhabit histories or think of history as a resource?

How are educators, artists, activists and intellectuals participating in the quest for solutions leading to a more equitable cultural production today?

Why is the field of cultural work still considered elite?

Is it true that collaboration is not always about putting together people in the same room?

How can we use cinema as a night school?

IN CONCLUSION

ARAC's practice will continue to evolve and multiply as new perspectives are introduced, old theories are revisited and challenged, and interactions with those from outside of our collective (by way of invited experts or observers and friends) reveal blind spots and hidden gems. We depend on this for our growth and therefore welcome it. More than anything, we embrace the call it presents to us to collaborate and exchange more extensively with others.

7

Massive thanks to Gudskul, fellow contributors and the Bauhaus Dessau Foundation.

Text by Lineo Segoete (Maseru working group)

An essay by Ola Uduku

Reading time 10′

Exile education environments in Nigeria and Tanzania

Since the beginning of the post-war era, the provision of education was a central feature of so-called development policies, with the United Nations declaring it second only to the right to life and shelter. This tenet, it can be argued, caused to standardise both educational methods and outcomes at a global level. By examining two projects from different parts of the African continent, it however becomes apparent that this standardised conception of education and its architectural envelopes, when applied to the spatial configuration of a learning environment, can help accommodate very different educational projects. Both institutions we are going to look at operated outside the public school system, and both have been established in order to cater to exile communities—albeit markedly distinctive ones. What this essay proposes is to analyse these institutions with regards to the ways in which their locations and constructed spaces influenced the lives of their users, thus illustrating how competing globalised networks and alliances in postcolonial, Cold War conditions played out on the school level.

INTERNATIONAL SCHOOL IBADAN, NIGERIA (1965)[1]

In the former British colonies of West Africa, the early 1960s were a transitional era during which the construction of infrastructure, of schools, hospitals and social housing changed from the oversight of colonial institutions to that of the newly formed nation states, namely Sierra Leone, Gambia, Ghana and Nigeria.

In the public construction paradigms of these countries, the building as envelope remains the symbol of modernity: the incorporation of the exterior had been actively discouraged as this was seen as a retrograde step, whereas new housing and institutional buildings such as hospitals and schools were supposed to lead the way toward a modern future as the purveyors of new living, medicine, education etc.

Separate from these state school building programmes, a number of schools were designed and constructed for children of expatriates and senior staff associated with certain companies and institutions. The International School Ibadan (ISI), designed in the early 1960s by the expatriate architectural practice Design Group Nigeria for the children of academics and senior staff associated with the emerging university college Ibadan, Nigeria, was planned for 450 pupils, taking into account tropical climatic design principles of the time as well as contemporary educational theories.[2]

As the architectural envelope for a wide-ranging curriculum, international pupils, staff and leadership, the ISI demonstrated the possibilities of contemporary institutional tropical design with significant public funding (coming from the University of Ibadan).

The ISI has always delivered a full, western-focused curriculum up to A-level standard, covering arts, science and specialist subjects such as music or technology. The classrooms were also designed to conform the norms of the British education system, with base classrooms for all classes and ancillary classrooms for science, music and other subjects. The classroom blocks were oriented to enable cross-ventilation and adequate shading to avoid overheating and direct glare. Of most interest is the open-air dining/social area which acknowledges the relative ambient climate conditions, allowing for 'inside-out-side' living. This is one of the earliest examples of climate-oriented design being directly applied to non-domestic, institutional spaces in Nigeria, with Arieh Sharon's 1966 plan for the main cafeteria area at the University of Ife taking this design approach to its full expression.

ISI's uniqueness in context and cost however limit its replicability—although it does deserve more publicity as a demonstration of the possibilities of good curriculum and appropriate, environmentally responsive, tropical school design.

SOLOMON MAHLANGU FREEDOM COLLEGE/DAKAWA DEVELOPMENT CENTRE, TANZANIA[3]

Whereas the ISI mainly catered to a relatively privileged group of exiles, the history of Somafco and Dakawa is inextricably linked to the struggle of the African National Congress (ANC) against the South African apartheid regime, and its militants seeking refuge and training in allied countries. It is remarkable that one of the main catalysts for the establishment of ANC settlements and schools outside South Africa was a call for educational justice, as thousands of Black South African school students took to the streets of

the Johannesburg township Soweto in 1976 to protest
the imposition of Afrikaans as the language of inst-
ruction. The South African government's brutal crack-
down on the Soweto uprising radicalised many
Black youths; they went abroad to join the ANC, which
had effectively been banned from operating inside
the country under the apartheid powers in 1960.

The ANC's reaction to the massacre consisted
in calling the world's attention to the atrocities of
the apartheid regime while at the same time negotiat-
ing with its allies on the African continent and beyond to help establishing strong ANC exile institutions,
with the goal of developing a phalanx of educated
cadres who would fight and strategise for a future ANC
government in a liberated South Africa. Close allies
such as Tanzania's leader Julius Nyerere were able to
provide safe passage for ANC refugees to leave
South Africa. The agreement to set up residential
camps in exile was taken swiftly, with the blessing
of the UN and funding from various sources. It was
always to be a temporary measure, as the young
people fleeing were fully engaged with the ANC: most
were expected to go back to South Africa to continue with the struggle, whilst a few would and did
travel abroad on scholarships by institutions on
both sides of the 'iron curtain'.

With the blessings of Julius Nyerere, the group
of ANC members who had arrived over previous
years as exiles and refugees from the ongoing violence in South Africa were given a piece of land
in Mazimbu, a village on the outskirts of Morogoro, to

develop as a site for the proposed ANC educational and vocational training facility. The main design for the school classrooms and blocks bears strong similarities to the design plans as specified and popularised by UNESCO programmes since 1945. The buildings were functional and provided the basic necessities. Construction began in 1977, with substantial support from anti-apartheid activists both from Scandinavian countries and from socialist states. In 1979, the camp would be named 'Solomon Mahlangu Freedom College' (Somafco) in honour of the young ANC militant executed by the apartheid regime earlier that year. As the Somafco campus soon was at capacity due to the ongoing influx of South African youths, the Tanzanian government gifted a second site to the ANC near the village of Dakawa, where education mostly focused on basic competences as a prerequisite for militants to continue their studies at Somafco. Whereas most buildings were erected using brick-and-mortar construction methods, there have also been several experiments with prefab techniques in order to reduce building costs.

As some may query the education programme which remained within the conventional western-focused curriculum and could hardly be called revolutionary, this could be countered through the explanation that many students who went on to receive scholarships were expected to use the education acquired at Somafco and Dakawa to assimilate or adapt to the international education regime they would encounter abroad. Supported by allied African states and a network of solidarity movements in the East and the West, the ANC camps in Tanzania remain a unique case illustrating what could be achieved when politics and economics aligned: the establishment of educational infrastructure that would serve the South African liberation struggle. The camps successfully enabled lives be lived until South Africa was finally free. The architectural symbolism of this project, whilst extant in the memorials that exist to this increasingly distant past, takes a secondary position to the communities and lives that the ANC camps in Tanzania helped form and transform.

COMPETING GLOBALISATIONS

The ISI and Somafco/Dakawa rely on similar architectural approaches while at the same time being embedded in very different geopolitical networks. In spite of their differences, these networks are not mutually exclusive: the competing globalisations of the West and the East had a significant overlap, especially with regards to the international anti-apartheid solidarity movement.

Whereas the ISI continues to operate as a school associated with the University of Ibadan, and has achieved near-iconic status for its progressive design, in the case of Somafco/Dakawa it seems clear that the infrastructure built was secondary to the socio-political ambitions of the project. The former ANC camps nevertheless display some remarkable continuities in both regards up until this day. As apartheid was finally dismantled in South Africa in 1992, the Somafco and Dakawa settlements were returned to the Tanzanian government. The Somafco campus is now being used as the principal site of the Sokoine University of Agriculture, while the Dakawa complex houses a variety of educational facilities, such as a teachers college and a high school. The historical legacy of the ANC campus has also not been forgotten: the former main administration block has a plaque and memorial commemorating the campus' initial use. Moreover, the graves of ANC exiles who died on the campus remain tended in dedicated cemeteries on both sites. There are also regular visits by former ANC campus residents and other South African politicians to the campus, which thus became a symbol of the diplomatic ties of the two countries.

1   The project is first being reported upon in the journal *West Africa Builder and Architect*, Nov–Dec 1965, pp. 108–112.

2   Ibid.

3   For reference, see Seán Morrow. 'Dakawa Development Centre: An African National Congress Settlement in Tanzania, 1982-1992', in: *African Affairs*, 97/389, October 1998, pp. 497–521. http://www.jstor.org/stable/723343, accessed 15 June 2023. An even more comprehensive historiography is offered in Seán Morrow, Brown Maaba and Loyiso Pulumani. *Education in Exile: SOMAFCO, the ANC School in Tanzania*, 1978-1992. Cape Town: HSRC Publishing 2004.

Editors' note: This text is partly adapted from a talk that Ola Uduku gave at a symposium marking the opening of the exhibition *Doors of Learning. Microcosms of a Future South Africa*, developed in the context of the *Bauhaus Lab* programme in Global Modernism Studies, at the Bauhaus Building in August 2022. As an additional result of this programme, a homonymous anthology assessing the history of the ANC camps in Tanzania from a variety of perspectives has recently been published in the Bauhaus Paperbacks series by Spector Books. The essay also incorporates an edited excerpt of Ola's essay 'Responding to the Environment. Post-Independence Learning Spaces in West Africa', first published in German in: Tom Holert/HKW (eds.). *Bildungsschock. Lernen, Politik und Architektur in den 1960er und 1970er Jahren*. Berlin/Boston: De Gruyter, 2020. The excerpt is reprinted here with kind permission by Ola Uduku and Tom Holert.

8

Embracing
contingencies

9

Responding to a set of questions on the epistemological implications of decolonisation in the field of design within and beyond academia, Pedro Oliveira engages in an email conversation with Regina Bittner.

REGINA BITTNER Why is the design discipline in particular challenged to question its own epistemologies, its methods of knowledge production, its logics and its historiographies?

PEDRO OLIVEIRA I wouldn't say this is particular to the design discipline itself, although it is remarkable how, in the past few years, a specific kind of resistance to that questioning surfaced and still refuses to go away. That being said, I believe a lot of it relies on the ways in which what counts as 'knowledge' is constituted and perpetuated, namely as a discrete, mappable, and always measurable set of metrics through which what is considered to be reproducible and verifiable has precedence over the subjective, the serendipitous, the intuitive, the relational and the spiritual. That which is named 'design' is in fact only displaying what is elicited by its methods. In other words: in its desire to constrain, map, measure, quantify and reproduce, design can only account for its own designs and its ontological and epistemological limitations. Hence, it might be difficult to let go, to do away with the idea that designing, even in its (historical) attempt to free itself from the stark separation between hard and soft sciences, is still very much bound to extractive and measurable ways of producing and reproducing the colonial episteme. This is not separated from a certain degree of disciplinary narcissism, that is, the fear that by challenging the knowledge produced by design methods, we might dissolve the boundaries that distinguish design from other fields and methods and complicate the hubris of mastery that its own disciplinarity (or commitment to it) holds dear.

RB How can design be freed from its entanglement with western notions of universality?

PO First and foremost, by acknowledging its own role in not only reproducing, but also perpetuating these notions of universality in its own ethos. In the introduction to *Black Skin, White Masks*, Frantz Fanon has delineated the limits of methods, their inadequacy in addressing the social and psychological causes and consequences of a racialised way of being and doing in the world. For him, methods eventually "devour themselves". But I believe that what he said next is even more important: that this should be our only next logical starting point.[1] Designers have much to learn by engaging in non-extractive modes of doing that acknowledge local cosmologies and imaginaries. While it can be argued that recent attempts to 'decolonise' or 'pluriversalise' design have in a way begun to enact that, I have yet to see approaches that do not try to 'correct' or 'design' them anew. I say this because in my view (and that of many of my colleagues engaged in the same struggle) this requires a strong rejection of universality in favor of minor localisms, in favor of contingencies that are always already responding in relation to (and not referencing) the colonial episteme. Let me be clear: 'universality' is not a vector, but an enmeshed network, a fiction with material consequences that, like every other fiction, needs to be dealt with as such. So, the question we have to grapple with becomes: how do notions of universality complicate the designs of minor localisms, and how can other, minor, local, contextual and positional designs complicate—and eventually dismantle—colonial notions of universality?

9   **RB** How can we rethink the agency of design beyond the western solutionist and anthropocentric models?

PO Often it is the anxiety of the new that compels much of design thinking and doing, while I believe that there is a lot of work to be done to undo what buzzwords such as 'innovation' have brought about, which have silenced other voices and ways of being and doing. This takes us beyond questions of the 'human-centredness' so inherent to design knowledge over the past decades. I think that attention must be given not only to the anthropocentric ways of design, but also to design's own contribution to (and entanglement in) racial and racialised frameworks. It is, indeed, the very notion of a 'centre' that drives the thinking of 'centredness' to begin with, and that is so pervasive within the design discourse that we seldom question its own logics and grammar. But if design were considered from a relational standpoint, we would not only decentre (and dethrone) the 'human' and thus expose its construction as a referent to 'being' (or, if we follow Sylvia Wynter, the "overrepresentation of Man"[2]) but also simultaneously undo the exclusions that design has enacted on those who have not, historically and contemporarily, partaken in the notion of 'humanity'.

RB What alternative emancipatory approaches are addressed by practices and discourses on the decolonisation of design knowledge and design education?

PO I strongly believe that possible answers to this question—or engagements, because perhaps there is no way of giving a fixed or stable 'answer'—are not to be found in design. In fact, these might be answers that have been already given long ago, and we designers were simply not listening. Answers that were given to us by indigenous knowledges, by anticolonial struggles, by feminist revolutions, and so on. From the moment that we do away with the idea that 'decolonisation' is something new to design—or to any form of knowledge production for that matter—we begin to acknowledge what the epistemic devices of colonialism have sought to erase: namely, the idea that knowledge is not fixed, stable, not always measurable, not always universally applicable, and not always reduced to a short-term, packable sets of 'tools' or 'methods' that can be applied and exchanged, devoid of context and at will.

Thus, an emancipatory approach to design is committed to the forging of new alliances, ones that are intrinsically bound to the preservation of land, water, food, language, communities,[3] and to the larger project of decolonisation, that is, to paraphrase Denise Ferreira da Silva, to the restitution of the total value extracted from bodies, land and knowledge.[4] While this might seem an impossible project, its incommensurability should not be a precondition for not trying, for not enacting the minor gestures we need to move towards that direction.[5] These alliances have to, necessarily, enact the work of listening, the work of renewing, unsettling, and to remain ever incomplete, to productively engage with vulnerability and the relationality that weave this world together. This has to be a way of thinking that is liberated from any desire to fill gaps or to see knowledge as something to be extracted because even when 'learning from', designers often believe their work is to translate and/ or compartmentalise that into a reproducible, pub-lishable (i.e. sellable) method. So, in short, allow me to answer by being opaque: an emancipatory ap-proach to designing demands a non-designerly ap-proach to design.

1	Frantz Fanon. *Black Skin, White Masks.* London: Pluto Press, 1986, p. 14. First published in France as *Peau Noir, Masques Blanc.* Paris: Editions deu Seuil, 1952.
2	For Wynter, the concept of the rational-scientific "Man"—as white, male, cisgendered, etc.—as

the driving concept of and for humanity is the model through which the totality of knowledge is constituted: what she calls the "referent-we." For more on Wynter's dense thinking about how we construct the logics that govern ourselves, cf. Sylvia Wynter. 'Unsettling the Coloniality of Being/Power/Truth/Freedom: Towards the Human, After Man, Its Overrepresentation—An Argument', in: *The New Centennial Review,* vol. 3, no. 3, fall 2003, pp. 257-337.

3   I am here paraphrasing Tiara Roxanne in their keynote address to the *AI Anarchies Autumn School* in October 2022.

4   Denise Ferreira da Silva. *Unpayable Debt.* New York: Sternberg Press, 2022.

5   See e.g. Eve Tuck and K. Wayne Yang. 'Decolonization is not a Metaphor', in: *Decolonization,* vol. 1, no. 1, 2012, or Danah Abdulla and Pedro Vieira de Oliveira 'The Case for Minor Gestures' (forthcoming).

Products for people:
Design and the
discourse of
development

10

The idea of 'development' has preoccupied designers in India since the inception of the discipline of design in higher education in the 1960s. In the early decades after independence, the government of India played a powerful role in the life of its citizens to provide a better standard of living. But how was this discourse of national 'good' refracted through the lens of design practice? Or, to put it another way, how did designers make these imaginaries 'real' for themselves and for those they sought to influence through their practice? As early as 1958, American designers Charles and Ray Eames asked in their India Report: "There is much discussion, in India, about Standards of Living. To what degree is snobbery and pretension linked with standard of living? How much pretension can a young Republic afford? What does India ultimately desire? What do Indians desire for themselves and for India?"[1] So what did Indian designers want for the new republic?

This early phase reminds us that the exigencies of Cold War diplomacy played a key role in bringing particular ideas of good design to India. The Eames's visit was sponsored by the Ford Foundation, which also funded the tour in India of the MoMA exhibition entitled *Design Today in America and Europe*. The exhibition consisted of furniture and consumer products selected "to bring to the attention of the Indian public the aesthetic values of the west in largely machine-made, mass produced objects" and to "provide an inspiration to Indian manufacturers and craftsmen for a solution to the many new problems that confront them."[2] The foundation also supported the training of the National Institute of Design's (NID) early faculty members in Europe, leading to curricula and pedagogies adapted from the Bauhaus, Basel and Ulm schools of design, which were echoed in the Industrial Design Centre (IDC) as well.

Two decades later, a decisive answer to the Eames's questions emerged in the form of 13 case studies presented at the 1979 UNIDO-ICSID (United Nations Industrial Development Organisation/International Council of Societies of Industrial Design) *Design for Development* conference at Ahmedabad and Bombay (now Mumbai). Designed mostly by faculty members of the two host institutions, the NID, Ahmedabad, and the IDC, Bombay, the products ranged from the bicycle to farm equipment, from the wheelchair and post box to type designs in Indian languages, and from power tools and safety equipment for miners to latrines and craft interventions.

The professional practice at IDC and NID, exemplified by the case studies curated for the conference, shows us how faculty members were thinking about and responding to the reality that decolonisation had taken place in a pluralistic and largely rural society with long and continuous handicraft traditions and small-scale industrial manufacturing capabilities, as well as distinct cultural practices. In each case study, though only a few are discussed here, the product is viewed as not only a functional or aesthetic offering but also as a cultural intervention to address social conditions. Examined more closely, the products point to an emerging set of design ethics committed to ideas of dignity, safety and well-being of Indian people.

In March 1977, newspapers reported that several farm workers—men, women and young people—were admitted to hospital in the north Indian town of Hissar. Their hands had been cut off while threshing the winter harvest. The short threshing season and the urgency of getting produce to the market speedily had led to the farming community to dismantle safety features, leading to a "tragic confrontation between men and machines".[3] Moved by the newspaper report, the NID contacted the reporter and the Ministry of Agriculture, leading to the design of safer power threshers (Case 3—*Design for safety: Power threshers—A harvest of suffering*). The engagement with rural life and the suo moto recognition of a space for design intervention underlines the "social, cultural and political factors that influence the selection and way of solving the design problems."[4] This is echoed in the design of safety devices for miners (Case 4—*Design for human factors: Miners' safety devices*) which describes how protective gear needs to take into account the physical discomfort caused by India's hot temperatures and high humidity in the rainy season as well as miners' cultural practice of needing to spit after chewing betel leaves and talking while working.

Two of the thirteen case studies were contributed by community-based Gandhian organisations,

suggesting that design does not take place only in design schools, nor is it practiced by professionally trained designers alone. One demonstrated improved farm implements (Case 8—*Design for rural technology: Farm implements*) to ameliorate fatigue and drudgery, to save labour but not to replace the labourer, which can be produced by local blacksmiths and carpenters. This is a nuanced view of product design in a country with a large population, high unemployment and traditionally skilled communities. The other addressed a significant unsavoury aspect of India's society, the caste system, in which one section of society is forced to manually dispose of human waste (Case 9—*Design for human dignity: The problem of Indian latrines*). The solution is a ceramic squatting latrine that can be flushed with a minimum of water into a pit where the waste is later
10 available as manure. Here, product design transcends functionality to become an instrument of transforming an inhuman social practice.

Castes are occupational groups and the discrimination perpetrated by the caste system is accompanied by the skills and knowledge held by each caste. In a drought-prone district in North India, textile and product designers worked with weavers and leather workers to create new products for urban markets (Case 12—*Design for rural progress: Learning for development at Jawaja*). The tension implicit in taking these design directions is not lost on the designers or design educators. In 1977, at the ICSID conference in Dublin, the NID's director Ashoke Chatterjee had

107

remarked that, "design as we teach it may stress the needs of westernised, affluent communities in urban India, increasing their own alienation from Indian society" and pointed to challenges that "demand a reappraisal of the disciplines and curricula which we imported from the west to transplant into our ancient and problematic soil".[5] The limits of importing philosophies, pedagogies and practices from Europe and America was also well understood in IDC faculty member A G Rao's comment: "The experiences in the West can only give us leads, and unless an approach appropriate to deal with the development problems rooted in social, cultural and political structures is developed, the profession would remain a white elephant."[6]

Exhibitions of Indian products were arranged at both venues. At Ahmedabad it was "a cross-section of products manufactured in village, small-scale, medium-scale and large industries" illustrating "the skills, materials and manufacturing facilities available in our country as well as some of our more important design challenges",[7] open to conference delegates and invited guests. At Bombay, it was a display of products designed at the IDC, and a publication entitled *Industrial Design Centre: A decade of design experience* describing these efforts was released in the presence of delegates. The IDC had earlier displayed its achievements along with the efforts of the members of the Society of Industrial Designers of India in a show entitled *Products for people* in order to "expose the public and industries to the potentialities of design".[8] Mounted at a prominent art gallery in the city, the exhibition was seen by more than 6'000 visitors.

Hosting the UNIDO-ICSID meeting and presenting the 13 case studies gave Indian designers space to engage with both local and international audiences to forge a place for design practice in the emerging postcolonial order. With some they shared a common colonial past which was responsible for their status of being 'developing countries' and they hoped their experiences would be of value to them all. While not explicitly pointing out the role of the developed world in the situation, the *Ahmedabad Declaration on Industrial Design for Development* adopted at the conference asserted that "designers in every part of the world must work to evolve a new value system which dissolves the disastrous divisions between the worlds of waste and want, preserves the identity of peoples and attends the priority areas of need for the vast majority of mankind".[9]

1	Charles and Ray Eames. *India Report*. Ahmedabad: National Institute of Design, 1958, p. 14.
2	René d'Harnoncourt. *Design today in America and Europe*. New Delhi: National Small Industries Corporation and Ministry of Commerce and Industry, Government of India, 1958, p. 4–5.
3	S. Balaram. *Role of Industrial Design: 13 Case Studies*. Ahmedabad: National Institute of Design, 1979, p. 8.
4	A. G. Rao. *Industrial Design Centre: A decade of design experience*. Bombay: Industrial Design Centre, 1979, p. 7.
5	Ashoke Chatterjee. 'Design in Developing Societies —Problems of Relevance', in background pa-

pers for the UNIDO-ICSID *Design for Development* conference. Ahmedabad: National Institute of Design, 1979.

6   Rao (as note 4), p. 7.

7   Anon. Exhibition catalogue in background papers for the UNIDO-ICSID *Design for Development* conference. Ahmedabad: National Institute of Design, 1979.

8   Rao (as note 4), p. 83.

9   *Ahmedabad Declaration on Industrial Design for Development*, point 16, Ahmedabad: National Institute of Design, 1979.

10

"An elephant on the eyelid is invisible, an ant across the ocean is visible": Learning design from akal-akalan practice archives

11

UNCONDITIONAL DESIGN AS A PRACTICE OF ARCHIVING AND TRANSFERRING DESIGN KNOWLEDGE

The desire to continuously explore and to make new discoveries has existed since there have been humans, and it is safe to say that design has also existed as long as humans have. This, however, often goes unnoticed. As a result, some people argue that product design has only been around since modern times and is thus part of a modern or western lifestyle.

The term 'unconditional design', which can alternatively be translated as 'unconditional planning', describes the (renewed) design of a product, the main function of which has undergone change as a result of the creative process of the human mind with regard to the usefulness of that product. This topic is unpopular in the field of art and design academia because it is thought to lack a specific standard or reference point to discuss its methods and further regulate or study this practice. We do not know when humans began to change the primary function of a product after it outlived its original purpose or began to repurpose products by converting them as needed, influenced and encouraged by specific situations and conditions.

These adaptations are highly influenced by their originators' creativity, experience, culture, needs, society, economy and environment. This causes the functional conversions to have different embodiments or design techniques from one region to another.

11

A new kind of creative process among citizens without prior design knowledge or design education, aiming to create designs with novel functions, has become a popular form of expression. In 2017, we finally decided to create the *UnconditionalDesign* platform on Instagram to collect the results. This platform is operated by the ruru ArtLab team and enables us to dissect the findings in a light-hearted way with product design discussions on each product shown. The project has expanded to several cities in Indonesia and has become a medium to channel contributions in the form of photos and videos using the hashtag #akalakalanwarga ('common sense') in each city or region.

As the UnconditionalDesign project expands, it becomes more visible in the form of knowledge exchanged through contributions on Instagram as well as stories about how a product is adapted before it is used. We also exchange knowledge in talks with people in the general community as well as academics. UnconditionalDesign also opens up cross-disciplinary collaborations to discuss or make collaborative practices more challenging using unusual, neglected forms of programmes such as workshops, seminars, joint exhibitions, and interventions in public spaces.

Starting with a collaboration with Stuffo, we conducted the first unconditional design workshop, titled *Cooking Objects*, for participants at Gudang Sarinah, South Jakarta. The workshop was the first unconditional design inquiry to experiment with the knowledge of the participants, who were given a time and a location and were free to make anything using the available tools. All the workshop materials were unused objects, readily available around the site.

The second unconditional design trial was a collaboration with LabTanya, a short course titled *Saturday Sunday Design Learning* (SSDL). We conducted meetings every weekend with the participants at the LabTanya studio, providing a brief reading or design research assignment that was presented, discussed together, then investigated.

Our collaboration with LabTanya continues with a programme we initiated in the city of South Tangerang. *Fraktal City* is an inter- and transdisciplinary experimental platform that involves and connects communities of residents with various challenges as well as problems in everyday life through the medium of design.

This programme invited fifteen young designers, architects, artists or makers to collaborate with ten young people from five sites (villages and housing complexes) in South Tangerang for a month, forming an experimental laboratory and responding to topics linked under the title *Material Connects* at individual sites. As a provision of the experiment, the participants are supported throughout by facilitators and a series of classes, workshops and discussions.

As a way to disseminate and celebrate the knowledge that was successfully produced throughout the programme, the experimental results of the participants will be displayed in exhibition activities including a series of public programmes, discussions

11

The term 'unconditional desig' describes the (renewed) design of a product, the main function of which has undergone change as a result of the creative process of the human mind with regard to the usefulness of that product.

and open lab activities (open experiments). Subsequently, each community site will be turned into a subject and design laboratory.

For a month, each team will map and reinterpret everyday life in their respective environments, finding things that can be used as tools to restore, rebuild or transform various possible forms of social and ecological relationships that exist in their communities. Experimental outputs are not limited to goods or products, but can also be systems, activity programmes or something else.

Following the joint initiative, the Unconditional-Design project was given the opportunity to participate in a residency, responding to and elaborating on ideas with the community of residents in the city of South Tangerang. Collaboration on a reading space

11

in the selected village location and discussing and carrying out experiments together with the local community are among the proposed initiatives.

Making recordings of the memories of residents about spaces and objects in their daily lives over the past few years has also become a tool enabling interaction together in the village space. Through the observation, historical investigation and tracing of village narratives, the Jawara Waste Bank community, in collaboration with the UnconditionalDesign project, tried to reactivate and adapt some of the residents' unique pastimes in the remaining spaces.

OPEN-SOURCE RESEARCH PROJECT

The use of social media by the UnconditionalDesign project is one way to transfer and redistribute information collected independently, creating an open-source project on Instagram. This design research project is still ongoing today, finding an extension to the role of the people's imagination in the city and in the interior of the village. The project stores the data in an archive of findings and categorises them according to the type of product design, material, additional functional purposes, and space, which is the ideal approach to adopt.

Contributors who send photos of objects are also given the opportunity to discuss their findings, the results of which serve as descriptions for their posts. In this way, they discover new opportunities and points of view from reading about methods or inventive approaches and discussing them. Often, any knowledge about how a product of citizen-led repurposing becomes a functional form is not recorded or visually described because it is only exchanged orally between residents.

11

Archive as a site for knowledge exchange

12

ÖZGE ERSOY We met the participants of this publication through Gudskul and documenta fifteen.

Asia Art Archive's recent collaboration with Gudskul and our contribution to documenta fifteen build on our ongoing research on the role of academic and alternative pedagogy in the development of contemporary art in Asia.

We received ruangrupa's invitation to become part of a group of collectives focusing on education. The initial question was how we, as an art archive, could contribute to discussions about knowledge sharing in the cultural field. Asia Art Archive (AAA) is a non-profit organisation initiated in 2000 to respond to the need to document the various recent histories of art in this region. We have an onsite library in Hong Kong, and we have a growing repository of primary source material, photographic documentation, video recordings, ephemera and more, which we digitise and make accessible for users worldwide— they are all freely accessible on our website. These materials are related to artists who are not only creators of artworks but who are educators, organisers, curators or writers at the same time, so when you look at their archives, you don't only see materials about a single artist but you can also relate to changes, fluctuations and discussions in the cultural communities they have been part of.

For our contribution to documenta fifteen, we highlighted the work of a group of artists committed to preserving cultural memory through their work and pedagogy. We focused on the following collective endeavours: the artists associated with the faculty of fine arts at Maharaja Sayajirao University of Baroda, India, and the Living Traditions movement in post-independent India; the feminist collective *Womanifesto* that organised biennial events in Thailand between the mid-1990s and mid-2000s; and performance artists who used everyday objects and sites, documented each other's work and participated in performance festivals in East and Southeast Asia from the 1990s onward.

The title of our display, *Translations, Expansions*, hints at how these artists study, document and rein-terpret knowledge that is part of daily life—the verna-cular and the often overlooked types of knowledge beyond textual knowledge or what we learn at school. They absorb these forms into their work and peda-gogy and pass them on to next generations in a trans-formed state. This is different from the traditional understanding of cultural preservation and informs the work we do as an archive: our goal is to build resources and keep activating them at the same time. This is why it's crucial for us to engage artists, re-searchers and educators to interpret our resources and promote debate around our shared research interests.

SUSANNA CHUNG As an art archive, we contributed to documenta fifteen thanks to an intiative of Gud-skul. Our collaboration with the knowledge-sharing platform Gudskul—our most recent project in Hong Kong—is a way to give back: this time, we invite contemporary art collectives to engage with an archive, most specifically with the archival resources we have on art collectives in Asia. Titled *The Collective School*, this project explores artist-driven, self-organised and collective models of learning. It began with our invitation for Gudskul in 2020. The platform in turn invited eight collectives from across Asia to join the exhibition—they are also contributors to this publication. In the exhibition, we see their artistic responses to archival materials such as videos, sculptures, games and zines, which we developed together through group conversations over the past year.

We are excited that *The Collective School* is the inaugural exhibition in our newly renovated library in Hong Kong. Located in a library rather than in a white cube gallery space, this exhibition also reflects our way of seeing archives and libraries as social spaces to connect people, to share and exchange knowledge. Instead of building a static archive waiting to be discovered, we actively organise exhibitions, talks and workshops around our research and urgent topics in recent art in Asia.

ÖE We develop research programmes as well. In the past two years, I was particularly excited about *Life Lessons,* a series of conversations we organised with more than twenty artists who teach at universities, build educational programmes at arts organisations or run their own schools. The last conversation in the series was about school as a form of intervention.

Noor Abed and Lara Khaldi spoke about the *School of Intrusions,* a peer-led, mobile learning platform that they co-founded in Ramallah in 2019. Ahmet Öğüt talked about the *Silent University,* which he initiated in 2012 as a solidarity-based knowledge exchange platform run by displaced people and forced migrants. These artist-led para-institutions make us question the potential of art institutions to address issues of social justice—distribution of opportunities and privileges. And now, with *The Collective School,* following Gudskul's model, we discuss how a school for collectives alters our understanding of art education models that often tend to focus on individual improvement. As always, we keep learning from artists.

Here it would be interesting to speak about how we have developed AAA's *Learning and Participation* (L&P) platform as this is a model where we learn from teachers and artist-educators.

SC The archive is not only a space for academic research, but also a catalyst for creative inquiry and practice. As a resource centre, we support teachers to become facilitators, develop teaching strategies to motivate students to get inspired by artists and AAA materials in order to create multi-layered works, be it artwork or writing.

L&P started in 2009, around the time of the visual art curriculum reform in Hong Kong. The reform requires students to develop a wide perspective of art across time and geographies. In order to support students to critically appreciate art in different cultural

125

contexts, teachers have to acquire knowledge in contemporary art, which they were lacking in professional training. We wanted to respond to this practical and immediate need. When we started, none of the Hong Kong museums or independent art organisations provided this type of educational support.

We have worked with different formats, methodologies and audiences in the last decade. For the first few years, our programmes were geared to young people aged 15 to 25. From 2012 onward, we have organised more educators' programmes to equip them with necessary knowledge in contemporary art. In 2017, with new contemporary art organisations entering the scene in Hong Kong with bigger teams and resources, AAA made a strategic decision to focus on teachers who can influence more students in the long run.

To support teachers, we develop programmes and online resources. For example, *Teaching Labs,* a series of talks and artist-led workshops, is designed to help teachers to discuss historical contexts, artistic practices and their current needs in education. And we develop online resources along with artists, researchers and teachers. We recently launched *Open Call: Artist Exercises,* an online project which brought together artist-educators and collectives from Malaysia, the Philippines, India, Singapore, Indonesia and Chinatown in Boston to develop creative exercises for their communities of learners, connecting AAA collections and their local context and educational environment. The participants carry out exercises

126

with their group of learners and put together artist exercises as resources for educators, which are accessible online for teachers and learners in the long run.

ÖE AAA currently works with teachers from more than 250 local schools in Hong Kong, who bring their students to the AAA Library to learn about contemporary art through our resources. This is a good point to speak about our communities. Hong Kong is our base, and our most immediate communities—artists, educators and researchers—are based here as well. Since the beginning of the organisation, however, we have been interested in creating a resource for contemporary art for Asia and making connections across different art scenes.

In 2004, art critic Lee Weng Choy wrote about what 'Asia' might mean. He says that 'Asian' as an "adjective often characterises something as Asian in its essence" and 'Asia' as a "complex, contested and constructed site." We refer to that with our name —Asia Art Archive. As a team, we are interested in looking for narratives beyond nation states, for artists who travel and contribute to different art scenes in the region, for shared and also divergent trajectories so as to contribute to a "more generous art history", as our co-founder and former executive director Claire Hsu puts it. This is why we continue to work with artists, educators and researchers as well as like-minded organisations in a larger region. *Mobile Library: Nepal* is a great example of this.

127

SC Yes indeed. The Mobile Library is an initiative we started in 2011. It seeks to give foundational support to universities and independent art initiatives by activating an itinerant library with educational programmes.

Building on past editions of the library in Vietnam, Sri Lanka and Myanmar, we recently collaborated with the Siddhartha Arts Foundation to provide reading materials to artists, students and educators in Kathmandu. The Mobile Library: Nepal was equipped with modular shelves, which enabled the project to adapt to different venues, ranging from universities to independent arts spaces. It became a social space for conversation, pop-up exhibitions, workshops, research and learning. We also developed a fellowship programme for art educators, where seven early-career art educators worked together for a year to make use of the materials in the library through a series of engagements with artists in the city and youth-led workshops for their peers.

As the library occupied unique spaces and infrastructures in Kathmandu, thanks to the people who activated the library, it was able to initiate conversations with other local libraries and archives in the area as well as the wider region in Asia. We would like to further build on this in the coming years. It has been encouraging to see the regional community address challenges in contemporary art education together. We hope to continue expanding these networks of knowledge sharing and collaboration.

A report by
Mayumi Hirano and Mark Salvatus (Load Na Dito)

Hanging school—School suspended

13

Kabit at Sabit is a 2019 exhibition by Load Na Dito. With the idea of holding future editions, we regard the exhibition as a learning process, an alternative form of school that enables salutary tensions between trial and error, theory and praxis.

This short essay sketches out our initial concept of Kabit at Sabit, the process of realising, reflecting and reimagining.

BACKGROUND AND OVERALL CONCEPT

Kabit at Sabit was conceived as a one-day, multi-site exhibition across the Philippine archipelago, continuing our critical exploration of methods of curating as a potential to generate sustainable local art ecologies. We found the open call approach best suited the curatorial aspiration for inter-dependency, for collective survival.

We disseminated the call on various social media platforms with one simple guideline: "Present an artwork/project on the exterior of your house or studio, on streets, or at other outdoor venues with easy access for the public on May 11, 2019." Taking place three days before the Philippine general election, during which public spaces and social media sites were bombarded with political campaigns, Kabit at Sabit also explored the expanded social sphere by playing with multiple layers of viewing experiences, both physical and virtual. We asked the participants to post photographs or live-stream videos of their work simultaneously on their social media sites with the hashtag #kabitatsabit. The participation was open to anyone in the field of art and culture; 32 individuals and groups responded to our call and joined the project.

Kabit is a Filipino word for 'being attached', 'connected', or 'fixed', and *sabit* is a Filipino word that roughly translates as 'to hang' or 'hanging', implying the temporariness and transformability of the material presence. The words also have layers of reference to social relationships. Thus, the exhibition Kabit at Sabit expressed our attempt to play with materials and with social conditions of vulnerability, insecurity and unpredictability.

Kabit at Sabit was inspired by the local, communal tradition of the annual *Pahiyas* festival in the small farming town of Lucban in Quezon, Philippines, where the residents deck or adorn the facades of their houses with their bountiful harvest. Aside from natural produce, the locals also display foods, crafts and anything that reflects the resident's life, such as vinyl records, teddy bear collections, books or bikes. The festival's origin dates to the pre-Spanish, 15th-century pagan ritual of offering harvests to the gods and goddesses of the land. It was converted into a Catholic religious celebration by introducing a patron saint for farmers.

Through modifications, transformations and shifts throughout time, Pahiyas now transcends its former identity as a doctrinal tradition imposed by the coloniser and has become a cultural practice that brings the community together by sharing creativity, skills, knowledge, food, time, humour, and care for each other.

133

The curator and artist, the late Raymundo Albano, described Pahiyas as an example of an authentic form of installation art in the Philippines. In the text 'Installation: A Case for Hangings', he discusses installation "as a case to get through our authentic selves" in connection to the Filipino local cultural and natural environments. "It may be that our innate sense of space is not a static perception of flatness but an experience of mobility, performance, body-participation, physical relation at its most cohesive form."[1]

The creatively participatory, experiential and spatial qualities of the local festival destabilise the modern western perspective and allow multiple perspectives to roam around slowly and gently interact with each other, engendering worlds. The artistic form of installation, enabling unconventional choices of mediums and methods of production, was also instrumental in regaining the immediacy of artistic expressions within the spaces of everyday life.

Kabit at Sabit aspired to criticise the centrality of an exhibition by problematising the concepts of location, duration, and public. The exhibition unfolded simultaneously in multiple geographical locations, loosely connected by the thematic signal of Kabit at Sabit.

The exhibition was also a critique of the idea of curatorial selection. There was no curatorial intervention in the artists' plans. Propelled by an intention to tweak the familiar tensions of the one curating and the ones curated, the exhibition was designed to operate on differences, a multiplicity of ideas and on pluralisms of artistic approaches without engaging in a curatorial habit of creating one unified voice to narrate and stabilise a particular way of 'reading' the artworks. The exhibition explored a way to keep artworks in direct attachment with the context of the production site.

REFLECTIONS AND REIMAGINATIONS FOR THE NEXT KABIT AT SABIT

13

1 Circulation, participation and inclusion

With the participation of 32 artists and groups in different locations, we believe the project successfully decentralises the viewing experiences. However, in retrospect, the dependency on social media to disseminate the open invitations limited the project's reach to the existing networks of direct and indirect friends, to within the strong ties of relationships. All the participants who responded to our call came from the art and culture field, which might be complicit in creating the perception of art as a hermetic discourse. In future, how can we disseminate the call to a wider range of people in different disciplines, generations and beliefs, including our neighbours? First, we must imagine the potential of traditional ways of disseminating information, such as printed materials, local broadcasting, and oral communication. For this, we aim to get the help of the participants of the previous edition of Kabit at Sabit. This might also help to open communication routes to counter the force of disinformation prevailing in our society.

2 Hybridity of the exhibition

Social media was used as a parallel exhibition site to explore the expanded social sphere engendered through constant switches between online and offline spaces. Videos and photographs showing the preparation stage, the work and the performance played a role in archiving and collating individual experiences and opened up shared social realities. Long-distance participations were linked using hashtags. Accidental crossings with #kabitatsabit posts on social networks in a nonlinear order prompted other artists spontaneous participation. Without relying on a command structure, the entirety of the exhibition manifested as unfixed and transformative formations of parasites, rather than an organising host. The hybridity triggered intimate, deceptive, sometimes inspirational and provocative encounters, and generated stories and energies with, around, or through families, neighbours, communities and strangers.

3 Interactions

What can we further share? Because each artist simultaneously exhibited their works in their own spaces, it was impossible for the participants or spectators to visit all the artworks over the course of the project. As our energy was also concentrated on the production and presentation of the exhibitions, we feel that we failed to facilitate more active interactions and engagements among the participants. By exchanging and learning from ideas and real experiences with each other, Kabit at Sabit may start functioning as a learning platform that enables the participants to share the energy to prepare, present, reflect on and plan for the next. The continuous process of interactions will create a shared imagination, foster care for each other, and generate a sense of co-ownership of Kabit at Sabit. It may be more accurate to imagine Kabit at Sabit as a space for mutual learning and for practising collective survival.

13

1   Raymundo Albano. 'Installation: A case for hangings', in: Patrick D. Flores (ed.), *Raymundo Albano. Texts*, Quezon City: Vargas Museum/ PCAN 2017, pp. 17–18, here p. 18. First published in *Philippine Art Supplement* 2/1, January to February 1981, pp. 2-3. https://pcan.org.ph/wp-content/uploads/2020/02/albano_web.pdf, accessed 12 June 2023.

The climbing ivy: Loosen the boundaries

That day, there was a massive explosion followed by a deafening boom. To some, explosions are breathtaking; to others, they can be fatal. What a peculiar situation. The decibel level of the explosion was sufficient to cause irreversible hearing loss. In other words, these people now have developed a tolerance for unpleasant sounds as well as the voices of people moaning and groaning about basic needs, matters of justice, and climate change, all of which were difficulties everyone faced at that time. A bubble forms between those exposed to the explosion and the unaffected populations.[1]

14   Meanwhile, tucked away in a quiet corner of the empty room, a small group of people was busily daydreaming.[2] An old worn-out couch becomes a nightly chat partner. Quietly singing a loud tune that lacks melody. Voice the disappointment of the reality that is happening. The dusty books were stacked in a disorganised way in another room as if they no longer held any allure. Certainly not due to a lack of interest or time. They're sick of reading about fictional utopia that have nothing to do with our realities.

Looking out of the dusty window, we'll be transported back ten years before the catastrophic explosion.[3] Those were the glorious days when we had all the 'time' instead of wealth to be stored in our pockets, bags, sacs, and wallets. A voice in the room said, "We are them, ten years ago …" Yes, it is true. The days when we skipped classes and looked for answers in different corners to satisfy our curiosities.

It's when choices, skills and knowledge sharing were available, and the sun shone brighter.

This episode is over, but history has a way of repeating itself. One can only hope that the same spirit can be recaptured once more before the big bang. Leftovers from the purchase of rice and internet credit are essential to survival. It may have sounded heroic, but they never considered themselves fighters against injustice. They merely wanted to create a home where people can gather and tell stories after a long day of exploring the world, searching for answers to all of life's mysteries.

14   There's no denying that their city is encircled by historic ivory towers left behind by the explorers.[4] Their structure is massive and imposing. No wonder they are still around even after being hit by forces of nature. The buildings are not the only things that last, but thoughts and ideas of an ideal world are deeply carved into the skull base of their devotees.

It's tragic. The explorers' presence at that time was like a demon, seizing everything from the land to spices to blood without remorse. They were blinded by the glimmering nature and were envious. They built this nation for their benefits, one by one, slowly but surely. Every infrastructure, from highways to plantations, hospitals to cemeteries, and housing to schools, was built to produce competent workers. The mark they made on society has lasted until today. It's time for this hierarchy to fall apart. One of the people sitting in the corner of the empty room yelled, "Arrrghhh ... I'm exhausted." Let's relive the wisdom of our forefathers to break free from the shackles of ignorance.

ING MADYO MANGUN KARSO[5]

The aftermath of the explosion didn't last long. A loud trumpet blast was a wake-up call, a signal for us to rise. We slowly realised that the world is not so rosy. Everyone there appeared distressed and terrified, hiding their emotions behind expressions of grim resignation. However, ivory towers are rising and becoming more exclusive and costly. Their illumination is like that of a lighthouse leading the way. And who exactly is this guidance meant for anyway?

Perhaps now is the time for us to act, hoping to burst the glorious bubble, despite knowing it will be difficult. Then they placed an old rug in the center of the deserted room. It has an inscription saying, „Here we are, let's unite." They gathered energy from their ageing bodies. Let's learn from the spores that grow on old walls and towering fences slowly until the fertile land sprouts shrubs and ferns that, at the very least, colour this soil. Although it is sometimes destroyed, it will grow back quickly.

1   The art boom phenomenon has occurred several times in Indonesia. It happened for the first time in the 80s, and the last time in 2007/2008. It impacts not only the economic sector but also the socio-cultural context of the art ecosystem. Rising market demand for artworks promotes artists' production, which is supported by numerous art events such as exhibitions, discussions and art fairs. The term 'art boom' refers to Sanento Yuliman's essay *Boom! Where has our paint-*

ing gone? He criticised the phenomenon of boosting artwork sales as leading to an 'impoverishment' of Indonesian painting.

2 These conditions exist outside the art market. Many small art groups continue to thrive outside the mainstream organically.

3 In the early 2000s, Bandung had several alternative spaces. They became hubs for knowledge exchange outside large educational institutions.

4 'Ivory tower' refers to a secluded place for people involved, for instance, in science and the arts that keep them away from any contact with reality. Here we refer to this expression also as a symbol of higher education institutions.

5 *Ing Madyo Mangun Karso*: 'Even amid a hectic life, an individual should be able to awaken or encourage passion'. The sentence refers to three key pillars of the *Taman Siswa* educational system, founded on July 3, 1922, by Ki Hajar Dewantara. Taman Siswa was born as a form of resistance to colonialism in Indonesia through education and culture. The other two principles are *I ng Ngarso Sung Tulodo* ('someone in the front sets an example') and *Tutwuri Handayani* ('someone in the back provides support'). These three mottos serve as the foundation of Indonesia's educational system.

14

Editors' note: To complement these notes, Omnikolektif invited Changkyu Lee to share his perspective on the collective's practice. You can find his text on the following pages.

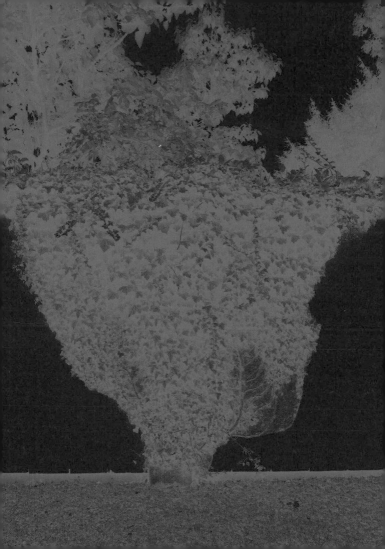

Decolonising the common: Beyond the dualism

15

Euro-American-centred aesthetics, a singular system of political economy or a transnational regime of virtue, is inadequate for engaging complex and dynamic conditions transforming global relations. With the rise of new art worlds such as Singapore and the Gulf States, we need to draw a new map of contemporary art worlds beyond the dualistic taxonomy and sensibilities of Euro-American aesthetics and 'Third World' aesthetics. Then, how can we understand the circulation of artists and artworks in interconnected mutuality beyond the binary pole of West/East and text/image? How do we position ourselves or participate in this global circulation and mobility? Do they have the potential to provoke new types of open, collaborative institutional and social structures?

During the fieldwork for my PhD dissertation in 2015, I started to get involved in Omnikolektif's project to 'answer' the anthropological questions, more significantly, to 'speak' to the global audience—mainly specialists in the art scene—through my research by addressing the 'Third World's' struggle and failure in the global art world. Rather than scrutinise the meaning and representation of contemporary Indonesian art as a passive result of expressive intentions, I have always focused on the materiality of Omni's artworks. By doing that, I have tried to address the predicament of 'Third World' artists' behaviour which is subject to a wide range of non-rational constraints. Walking along with Omni, I have learned how to loosen the boundaries instead of placing myself in the global hierarchy by proving: I can be a good loser.

Their short story sounds like an artist's egoistic self-reflection or hidden diary in the periphery. But ethnographically, Omni's project has enriched our understanding of how actors in the Indonesian art world translate the particularity of artworks into local knowledge by applying the aesthetic terminology and grammar of the global art world. Their projects also address the appropriations or predicaments that are created in that process as well. By following artists and artworks in their global circulation— at documenta, in their female-centred residency programme Masa Subur, or the concept exhibition format Getok Tular—Omni's projects reconsider the interconnected mutuality, rupture, and logic of the relocation and recreation of artworks in global circulation.

Aesthetic sensibilities create a new mode of perception and political subjectivity.[1] Omni's artistic experiments also still navigate a mechanism that translates the value of art, the sensibility and the aesthetics of the 'Third World' into the exchangeable. They want to know how this material/immaterial mediation influences the exhibition, managerial and performative practices of art, or how aesthetic dispositions are produced by this. Omni's projects also have been re-inviting the longstanding anthropological inquiry into gift exchange as a local place in which human relations are formed and where meanings of person, value and exchange are constantly in extension and retention.[2] As such, the ethnographic knowledge that will be produced by 'the common' and 'the audience' in Omni's project can also speak to a relatively unexplored object of inquiry for art history because it critically engages with interpretations of non-western reconfigurations of the global. The climbing ivy will glow and survive, not following human intention and logic but floating at the intersection of life's hybridity, hierarchy and contingency. *Ing Madyo Mangun Karso!* Omni's climbing roots go beyond dualism, finding a sustainable and fitting place to listen to others rather than enlighten the common.

1   Hans Belting, Andrea Buddensieg, Peter Weibel (eds.). *The Global Contemporary and the Rise of New Art Worlds,* Cambridge MA: MIT Press, 2013; Jacques Rancière. *The Politics of Aesthetics,* New York: Continuum, 2004.

2   Alfred Gell. *Art and Agency: An Anthropological Theory,* Oxford: Clarendon Press, 1998.

15

Editors' note: This text is a complement to the notes by Omnikolektif in the previous chapter (pp. 140–145).

Paradigms
and practices
of PRESISI

16

PRESISI is a programme based on a paradigm of students as independent individuals who study independently. The PRESISI programme aims to provide a choice of learning models, building on a habit of critical-analytical thinking, to deal with phenomena that exist around students. With this aim, PRESISI proposes a project-based contextual learning model, a form of learning that puts students and teachers in a position to experience direct interaction with their social and environmental situations and conditions. At the end of the process, the students will channel the outcome of their studies and the reflection on their experiences into work that is expressed through the medium of art.

PRESISI was initiated by three communities with a focus on pedagogy, namely Sanggar Anak Akar, Erudio Indonesia and Serrum-Gudskul, with support from the Directorate General of Culture of the Ministry of Education and Culture Indonesia. The programme has been implemented since 2020 in 100 schools in ten regencies and cities in various provinces of Indonesia: Aceh, Klaten, Karanganyar, Benoa, Kukar, Makassar, Maumere, Ternate, Ambon, and Jayapura.

The transcript below is a summary of viewpoints expressed during the focus group discussion OPRES SESSION #3 on 'Paradigms and practices of PRESISI', which was held on August 22, 2022, at the Gudskul Hall.

The focus group discussion participants were Andrea Aulia Rahmat, Angga Cipta, Angga Wijaya,

Aurelia Jessica Febiola, Balqis Prameswari, Dhitta Puti Sarasvati, Diah Rahmawati, Farelia Octa Viola, Hairun Nisa, Ibe Karyanto, Kaminah, Karina Adistiana, Lestia Primayanti, Moch Hasrul, M Sigit Budi S, Nadila Nindyta, Wacil Wahyudi, Wiratama, and Yuli Setiawati.

PARADIGMS AND PRACTICES
OF PRESISI

ANGGA WIJAYA PRESISI is implemented in areas with specific backgrounds. For example, schools in Aceh have a background as a conflict area, schools in Eastern Indonesia, too, but in addition these have the historical background of colonisation by the Portuguese. These social and historical backgrounds have an impact on the dynamics of education in each of these regions.

IBE KARYANTO Colonisation must be understood in the context of the hegemony of controlling consciousness through cultural works built by the colonialists. Ki Hajar Dewantara, who fought for independence, could not accept the fact that this nation is educated only with technical skills, meaning that education born from colonialism was nothing more than a teaching model to subjugate the Bumiputera so that they could meet colonial needs, both from a technocratic standpoint (mastery of administrative technology) and in the context of domination politics. The culture introduced to students at that time was born by colonial design. Thus, it is essential that, in educa-

153

tion, students have both freedom to choose certain things, and freedom from certain things. In terms of freedom to choose, we can approach students with the PRESISI model, and they can find the meaning of independence and how to use their freedom to learn. But to have freedom from certain things means to accept the heaviest burden because the weight the students bear is constructed by the force of ideological design. If we want to give students freedom from this, we must confront those forces.

KARINA ADISTIANA The ultimate goal is sovereignty, not just personal sovereignty, but the sovereignty of the state over its own resources, over its own knowledge. There is a lot of knowledge that is not distributed because it might be considered a nuisance to the current system. Is colonisation any good? Of course, it is! For certain groups! These really hold on to that power. There is no space for democracy in colonialism. While we ourselves claim to be a democratic country, a sovereign state, we are not. It's just that we don't get to feel it because in its current form, colonialism is not a threat backed by weapons.

IBE KARYANTO I am not aware of any history of decolonisation carried out by an organisation as strong as the state. Decolonisation is based on people who see, feel, experience oppression. If you have a vision for a movement for change, don't give up. This decolonisation will not be carried out like colonisation, which is the product of a strong and organised power system with all its capital: organisation, mass, finance, and so on. Colonisation in this new form exists and is included in the educational curriculum. Who has the knowledge? Who is in charge of that knowledge? Who has the authority to choose people in education? If the authorities are secure rulers pursuing certain interests, clearly this is a new form of colonialism in the current era.

LESTIA PRIMAYANTI Education is a colonial form, It is a very comfortable and romantic space. Therefore on introducing PRESISI as either a paradigm or a method in formal schools, at first it was perceived as a threat and uncomfortable. It's uncomfortable because we often come offering freedom, freedom from systemic pressure, freedom to explore learning, but teachers see that as a threat, thinking it shouldn't be like this, or not even knowing they are allowed to do that.

IBE KARYANTO PRESISI is not just a learning paradigm and model. As a movement for change, it must be able to stand alone and sustain itself. This is a design that is relevant for the decolonisation of education, not just once the project is completed. Colonisation is rooted in such a long history. The government, consciously or not, tends to still colonise the idea of education. Consequently, the decolonisation of education will develop if the people have a strong sense of solidarity. If we want to produce relevant knowledge in keeping with the social conditions around us, we must start from the reflections of stu-

155

dents on their social conditions and in the context of those conditions. They must be able to identify what may be a concern for the community and find a way and means to express those concerns.

WACIL WAHYUDI Western educational design likes to categorise things, so in Indonesia there are excellent schools, best schools, favourite schools, etc.

IBE KARYANTO Schools only provide knowledge that is relevant to capitalism, the point of which is to perpetuate it.

WIRATAMA We have the phenomenon of schools being labeled the best schools and elite schools with only certain people being privileged enough to be able to go there. The standard is very similar to that of the colonial system because there is a gap between the community having these privileges and those who do not have the necessary financial means.

16

HAIRUN NISA In elementary, middle, and high school, I went to school and followed all the teachers, orders, receiving lessons from the same book, with uniform learning methods. The teachers measured intelligence only according to certain abilities, such as exact knowledge. All the students had to understand the subjects without exception, get high scores to progress to the next school. The selection of a high school is based on economic capacity. If you come from a family that is economically capable, you can become a high school student. If you can't afford it, then you must choose a cheap private vocational school or *pesantren*, an Islamic boarding school, in the hope that, when you graduate, you can help the family's economic life by directly working.

DHITTA PUTI SARASVATI Students majoring in mathematics are taught based on mathematical theory. Of course, almost all the theory comes from the West. The question is: what happens when you are free to teach anything? Can we use our knowledge for a bigger purpose, for example towards a fairer world? We can teach numbers, fractions, but when we asked, for example, "How do farmers use mathematical reasoning for farming activities?" it became clear that we don't necessarily know the answer.

WACIL WAHYUDI Teachers are no longer the centre point of learning resources, but also act as facilitators, mediators and mentors. PRESISI also involves the surrounding environment as a study partner. Thus, there are no more students who are ranked first or superior. Based on that, how can students develop their potential and their environment so that both can grow together?

KARINA ADISTIANA PRESISI aims to encourage students and teachers to inquire and to question things that are not appropriate and not liberating, for example to question everything about the curriculum, the administration, and more.

157

LESTIA PRIMAYANTI Teachers and students finally found out for themselves, "Oh, this is what freedom means!" It didn't make them feel comfortable right away, they had to approach it and try it out slowly. Schools that have been implementing this method for two or three years are also still exploring true independence and creating a new system according to the relevance of their lives as schools in the community.

16

Learning in spite of the school

17

Responding to a set of questions on the epistemological implications of decolonisation in the field of design within and beyond academia, Nina Paim engages in an email conversation with Regina Bittner.

REGINA BITTNER Why is the design discipline in particular challenged to question its own epistemologies, its methods of knowledge production, its logics and its historiographies? How can design be freed from its entanglement with western notions of universality? How can we rethink design's agency beyond the western solutionist and anthropocentric model? What alternative emancipatory approaches are addressed by practices and discourses on the decolonisation of design knowledge and design education?

NINA PAIM Our world is deeply troubled, and design is fundamentally complicit in this. This is true whether we understand design as a self-contained discipline, as an academic and professional field, or whether we think of it more broadly as what humans do, which in turn designs (or shapes) us back. As a discipline, design is not neutral. It emerged in a specific time and place, namely 19th-century Europe, at the heart of the industrial revolution, and as the domain of elite white men. From its origin, this field has been inextricably entangled with western, capitalist and colonial heteropatriarchal modernity, and it serves to reiterate, reinforce and replicate these various systems of oppression. Even if we look at design more broadly, we'll also arrive at a similar conclusion. Our world is not 'naturally' unjust and un-equal; injustices are engendered into our world by design, by the powerful, by the oppressors. So how do we begin to undo them? I'm reluctant to provide any answers because I can only speak from my own experiences, which are inherently imperfect and incomplete. What follows might appear to be an exercise in self-exposure, but it is, rather, an attempt to listen to my body, my heart and my mind, and speak my truth.

Design was not my obvious first choice of career. Before arriving at this troubled field, I briefly studied economics at the Pontifical Catholic University of Rio de Janeiro (PUC-Rio), a private university located in an upper-class neighborhood of Rio de Janeiro in

Finding community is key to seeking liberation from any kind of harm.

Brazil. I left not because I disliked economics per se, but because the environment was sexist, racist, classist and homophobic. As a queer woman, my everyday life made me feel deeply othered. This didn't come exclusively from the curricula or the professors, but also—in fact, especially—from my daily interactions with my classmates. Essentially, I couldn't imagine them as my future peers, and I believe that some of them may have eventually found positions in president Jair Bolsonaro's far-right government. At the time, I left because I needed to find 'my people'. I share this experience to make two points: firstly, the problems we are discussing are not unique to design—they are systemic. Secondly, the violence and exclusions we face in the spaces we inhabit often change the entire trajectories of our lives. In the end, finding community is key to seeking liberation from any kind of harm.

After PUC-Rio, I enrolled in the design programme at the School of Industrial Design/Rio de Janeiro State University (ESDI/UERJ), which is a public institution with free tuition. In 2003, UERJ became the first university in Brazil to implement quotas for low-income, public school-educated, self-declared Black, brown and indigenous students. When I arrived there, these policies had already been in place for three years, and what had historically been a highly elitist space was already—though slowly—beginning to change. Oppressive hegemonic structures were still present, though significantly more on an institutional level than in my daily interactions with classmates, which, I must stress, were still conflictual. A snapshot of my class-

17   mates standing against the school's grey building shows a nonconforming bunch that often aroused reprimanding looks as we walked defiantly through the streets of Rio de Janeiro. With these peers, who often came from backgrounds that were very different from my comfortable middle-class upbringing, I began to organise myself politically, unaware of how this experience would later impact my life.

At the time, ESDI offered a five-year general programme that framed design as an all-encompassing, problem-solving discipline (notably, the curriculum has since undergone reform). As designers-in-the-making, we were taught that we could shape things of all scales and levels of complexity. From trains to coffee cups, pictograms to political campaigns, nothing seemed off-limits to us as omnipotent designers-to-be. But there was a disconnect between what we learned in the classroom and the deeply unequal Brazilian reality, constantly seeping, and sometimes pouring, through the cracks in the school's veneer. The curriculum was a steamroller: long days followed by long nights, bookending afternoons of exhausting manual labor in the school's workshops. As designers-in-training, we had to be 'formed', which meant we had to conform to fit in. We were plastic materials to be moulded, which often required us to be broken down and reshaped again. This was mentally, physically, intellectually and spiritually draining. To finish an assignment, I remember once

I started facing my bookshelf and looking
for the voices that weren't there, realising that
silences, indeed, speak volumes.

taking a block of resin into the shower so that I could
continue painstakingly sanding the material while
also attending to my bodily needs, my own tears blend-
ing with the cocktail of water and residue as it all
swirled away down the drain.

A fellow graduate from ESDI, Leonardo
Vasconcellos, who joined the school shortly after I
left, has described a similar experience of being
"broken down" by the school in a recent text published on *Futuress*, the feminist platform for 'designed
politics' that I co-founded and currently co-direct. The
term, coined by the design scholar Mahmoud
Keshavarz, attempts to make visible the integral bond
between these two deeply entangled fields: design
and politics. In his text, Leonardo describes the heart-

breaking process of being shattered and decon-
structed by design pedagogy and having to seek alternative ways to recompose himself outside the
school. Much like him, I wasn't aware of the implicit
politics surreptitiously being slipped under my skin
by the design curriculum, and I later had to confront
them through a painful process of unlearning—but
more on that later.

Of course, neither my generation nor Leonardo's
accepted any of this passively. Over lunches, coffee
breaks and chats as we strolled through the corridors,
friendships were formed through which we imagined other possibilities for the school and for design.
I was part of the group of students that initiated the
academic union at the school, named after Carmen
Portinho, a feminist activist and the first woman in
Brazil to receive the title of 'urbanist'. I was also a student representative, and I helped organise surveys
to fight some institutional problems we faced, including collecting complaints about harassment and
abuse by teachers, and bringing public awareness
to the internal theft of hundreds of books from the
school's library. We pooled our resources to organise
workshops, we teamed up to curate exhibitions,
we banded together to plan parties, and we joined
forces to co-edit publications, often in collaboration with teachers who became our allies. My first curatorial experiment, co-organised with two classmates, was a series of lectures titled *Design through
the looking glass.* For a whole week, we invited designers and non-designers such as anthropologists,

musicians, philosophers and filmmakers to sit side by side and engage in a dialogue across their differences.

Although this would become the seed of my future practice, at that time, none of this was deliberate or conscious; those experiments and acts emerged from our individual and collective struggles and desires. By the time I reached my final year, despite having calluses and scars on my hands, I was convinced that I hadn't been properly 'formed', so I decided to go on an exchange programme for a semester abroad. In the Netherlands, away from home, entangled in a much more individualistic environment, but with new peers from different corners of the world who quickly became close friends, I realised how much organising had become foundational to my understanding of design. This is something I learned inside the school, but despite the school. Migrating also produced new processes of 'othering' and new pressures to conform, pushing me to seek others in similar positions. Though I eventually fully transferred my studies to Amsterdam, my graduation project, co-initiated with my long-time Brazilian friend Clara Meliande, was an attempt to create bridges between these two worlds. It materialised as a temporary, free-of-charge design school at the heart of Rio de Janeiro, bringing together over 100 participants from Brazil and the Netherlands.

After graduation, I slowly moved from design to curating and editing, working with various mediating formats such as exhibitions, publications, workshops, and more recently, texts. Much like Leonardo describes in his Futuress text, I started facing my book-shelf and looking for the voices that weren't there, realising that silences, indeed, speak volumes. Suddenly, I could hear a myriad of burning questions that had been there all along, suffocated into muffled echoes and background noise. I first had to learn how to properly listen to the pounding beat of a 'why' stuck deep in my throat, stifled in my body, muted in my fingers—voices that were indeed desperate to speak. Exercising this critical consciousness made me question my references, preferences and thought structures. Oppressive systems that sustain and perpetuate western, capitalist and colonial heteropa-triarchal modernity are structural and structuring, they exist within us, inside us, all around us. Challeng-ing design's epistemologies, methods and histories became a painful process of unlearning, disentangling, and seeking new alliances. It is a change I'm still going through, and will likely continue for the rest of my life.

It's been twelve years since I left Brazil for what I initially thought would be a mere six months. Since then, I've moved countries four times, and since January 2022, I've found myself in yet another new context: Portugal. These multiple migration process-es forced me again and again to have to 'find my people', which has not always been easy, and often resulted in long stretches of solitude. But these difficulties and sorrows have also helped me meet others with whom to think and act. I cannot stress enough how much gaining critical consciousness, or *conscientização*, to borrow the term from the Brazilian philosopher Paulo Freire, cannot be achieved individually. It's not about self-improvement or self-actualisation, two tendencies that seem so prevailing in neoliberal design, but about a real transformation through dialogues across differences. Ultimately, liberation is not something that can be bestowed or given, but something that we can only achieve collectively, together, as lifelong student-teachers, forever incomplete, continuously willing to pose questions to which we might not find any answers. In the end, sometimes, the answer might begin, like this brief text, by redefining the terms of the conversation altogether.

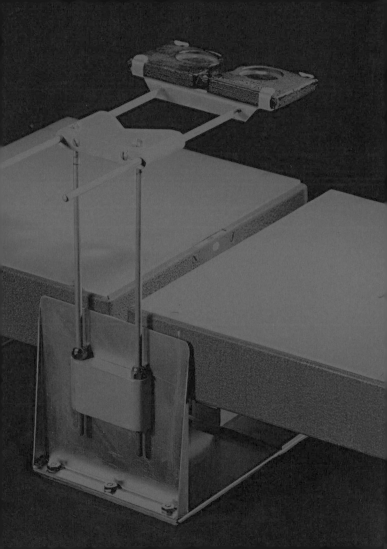

By Offshore (Isabel Seiffert and Christoph Miler)

Intertwingled pedagogies: A note to the monolith

18

In spring 2021, Offshore was commissioned by the Bauhaus Dessau Foundation to develop what was then called „a digital platform mapping art and design pedagogies beyond the Bauhaus". The brief read, in part: "Against the mode of a narrative of 'influences' that starts from the assumption of the Bauhaus as a 'centre' and its movement into the non-European 'periphery', diverse and multidimensional intercon-nections should become visible. Contrary to the noti-on of a self-contained Bauhaus teaching concept that has been applied as a model in different schools, the reading proposed here is that of a heteroge-neous conglomerate of pedagogical approaches, con-stantly changing in the course of its translations in different contexts." Here, Offshore responds to this brief after the launch of the website in late 2022.

DEAR BAUHAUS,

thank you for getting in touch and considering us for this project. We read your letter with great excite-ment and feel intrigued by your invitation to "map the ramifications of the Bauhaus pedagogy after 1933". As you might imagine, it will be a challenge to design a web platform for this rather ambitious endeavour, but we are more than happy to take it on. Please find our signature on the contract attached.

In eager anticipation of our first meeting, we want to start this journey with a personal anecdote already. Hopefully, this helps you to peep into our way of thinking.

If we remember correctly, we were nerdy first-year students at art academy, about to receive one of our first assignments. Our teacher asked us to create a family of abstract geometric signs, graphic symbols really, by using analogue tools only. Equipped with ink pens, rulers and graph paper we got our hands dirty and transformed the bodies of circles, squares and triangles rigorously. Working on their black and white shapes made us aware of composition and negative space, while their shimmering high-contrast edges sporadically caused visual vertigos. It is fair to say that this was fun, too. At least for a couple of classes. Until we learned that this assignment wasn't to last only for a few weeks, but for the whole semester. After all, this was a version of The Bauhaus Model, as our teacher would say. And so he expected to see not only a handful, but hundreds of hand-drawn symbols, rendered with computer-like precision by the end of it. Whenever a student was moaning too loudly about the imposed agony, he would respond: "Don't complain, you are developing a feeling for rational, timeless shapes and an archive of soon-to-be logos!"

This was back in 2008—and the global financial crisis was in full swing, with its bursting bubbles, bankrupt home buyers and non-stop mass layoffs. Following the news, we saw images of the banks and rating agencies that were to be blamed for the disaster. Irritatingly, their oversized logos on shiny facades and sky-high rooftops were bearing great resemblance to the symbols we were drawing in class.

175

Abstract, clean, geometric shapes. Against the visual backdrop of an insane global financial industry our "soon-to-be logos" didn't look quite so "rational" anymore. We can't recall why we never spoke about this in class, nor why our teacher kept dead quiet about

18 it. Still, it might have been during these months when we sensed for the first time that your rational ideals did not necessarily beget the utopias you had envisioned. Instead, it seems like your pedagogies and practices are rather "deeply complicit in many structural systems of oppression" as researcher Claudia Mareis and educator-activist Nina Paim observe.[1]

Rest assured: we don't want to step on your toes with this anecdote. Indeed, ask any designer of our generation about the Bauhaus and a few positive glimpses and awe for key figures will be on the table —from Anni Albers to Paul Klee, from Wassily Kandinsky to László Moholy-Nagy. However, as we reflect on our relationship with you, it was moments of friction and crises like the one of 2008 that made us question your and other omniscient design dogmas that are built for eternity. In our humble view, the world was always too pluralistic, complex and contradictory for such static, hegemonic horizons. As a result, we—in our double-role as designers and educators—are continuously trying to unlearn and reimagine your rigid rules.

This dip into the past might help you to understand how enthused we were when we received your brief. What a pleasure to hear that you want to scrutinise the myth of a monolithic Bauhaus model, composed of timeless and universal truths! And you might agree with us when we point to the views of Brazilian educator Paulo Freire. He, too, argued against an all-wise, static pedagogy when he wrote that "knowledge emerges only through invention and re-invention, through the restless, impatient, continuing, hopeful inquiry human beings pursue in the world, with the world, and with each other."[2] We couldn't agree more.

Naturally, such pluralistic modes of knowledge production have infiltrated your pedagogy in manifold ways. In fact, the rigid image of THE Bauhaus model is an illusion. Over the last decades you have been distorted, deformed and destroyed, hacked, hated and loved, cracked, smashed and reconstructed a billion times. An ever-changing conglomerate of heterogenous educational impulses would likely be a better description of your nature over time. Without a doubt then, the fragments of your pedagogical aftermath are not gone. Instead, they hurry-scurry in a dense and multi-dimensional web of educational practices until today.

Obviously, this densely entangled net is not easy to map. How can one shed light on all its threads throughout space and history? How shall we trace its ever-changing architecture, nodes and inhabitants that, to cite your brief, "do not follow the idea of a chronological sequence of past, present and future, but move between different geographies, times and cultures"?[3] How shall we map this fungi-like,

> We are aware that what follows might sound somewhat anachronistic and strange even—but we are serious—for as the core of it forms the *light table*.

decentralised, non-linear longue durée of knowledge production, and how to access all the relations that exist within it?

As we discussed these questions, we were hit by an idea. While still in its early stages, it nevertheless might provide a basic strategy to disentangle your web. We are aware that what follows might sound somewhat anachronistic and strange even—but we are serious—for as the core of it forms the *light table*.

Have you ever noticed what an ingenious research tool a light-table is? In the past it was used to review film negatives, or to copy designs for cartoons, animations, architecture and fashion. Sometimes, it was also deployed to analyse fish ovaries, examine leaf structures or interpret aerial photographs taken by military Tomcat squadrons.[4] Today, the light table might be considered an object on the brink of extinction, but it still fascinates. For it enables to order, examine, trace and arrange objects on its unpretentious surface. You turn on the lights and all of a sudden, a passive, dark space becomes an illuminated, active surface that allows to observe and arrange freely. There are no prewritten narratives, no ingrained hierarchies, no rules. It enables to drag in and drag out as you wish, examine and juxtapose forms, objects and images, compose sequences, and discover relationships. Now, allow us to imagine for a moment that we could apply such non-linear methods of investigation not only to photographs, drawings or fish, but indeed to your educational web. Wouldn't it equally allow to expose, examine and investigate its nodes, arrangements and interdependencies, thereby seeing otherwise invisible narratives?

In our view, a digital space inspired by the working methods of a light table would illuminate your entanglements with the world. Almost akin to the work of American conceptual artist Mark Lombardi, whose large-scale drawings shone light onto shady power structures by visualizing the relationships of politicians, multinational corporations and criminal organisations in a graphic way. He called them 'narrative structures'. They became so elaborate that journalists, and supposedly even the FBI, used them for their investigations.[5]

We are not sure if we want to stimulate the interest of Europol with our mapping endeavour, but we think Lombardi's way of working might serve as a great starting point. Powerful opportunities will open up when isolated bits of information are linked to bigger stories within a complex network of interdependencies, like yours. Of course, Lombardi created his links in an analogue way, simple lines on paper situated between names. On the contrary, our project will exist within the digital realm. Here, the pendrawn line of Lombardi is elevated to a hyperlink, while names and places are transformed into tags, folders and metadata. The sum of those related digital elements holds, like Lombardi's canvas, myriad narratives and knowledges that wait to be found.

Ted Nelson, the inventor of the hyperlink, famously coined the term 'intertwingularity' to describe the idea that all knowledge in the universe is deeply interconnected.[6] We think this is not only beautiful, but more importantly, we think this is true. No doubt, knowledge comes with power structures, but at the same time it is always relational, nested and entangled; it flows through time, space and bodies, even to the point of confusion. This is why also your pedagogy is deeply intertwingled. And we hope you agree that your intertwingled educational web could be examined, exposed and enriched on a digital light table. By illuminating your manifold threads and connections with other schools, actors, objects and ideas, unknown relationships and narrative structures might emerge on its surface.

Finally, allow us to express a word of warning: Seeing other systems of thought that run through your monolithic walls might shake your foundations a bit. Maybe you will be surprised, irritated and scared by what you learn. Maybe this will feel a bit destabilising. A bit like leaving the safe walls of your building to enter a confusing mixture of pasts, presents and futures. In these plurivocal spaces you might discover unknown connections and learn new things about yourself. And maybe—to borrow the hopeful words of bell hooks[7]—our endeavour will even allow you to forget that self and, through ideas, reinvent yourself.

We are looking forward to our first meeting.
Sincerely yours,
Offshore

1	Claudia Mareis and Nina Paim. *Design Struggles. Intersecting Histories, Pedagogies and Perspectives* (PLURAL) Amsterdam: Valiz, 2021, p. 11.
2	Paulo Freire. *Pedagogy of the Oppressed.* New York: Continuum Books, 2005, p. 72.
3	Stiftung Bauhaus Dessau. *Schulen des Aufbruchs: Angebotsanforderung*, document, Dessau,2021.
4	Wikimedia Commons image collection of light tables: https://commons.wikimedia.org/wiki/Category:Light_tables?uselang=de, accessed 1 February 2023.
5	Mareike Wegener. *Mark Lombardi–Kunst und Konspiration.* documentary film. Germany: Arte, 2012.
6	Theodor H. Nelson. *Computer Lib.* South Bend, 1974, p. 45.
7	bell hooks. *Teaching to Transgress. Education as the Practice of Freedom.* New York/London: Routledge, 1994, p. 3.

REGINA BITTNER

P. 7 Regina Bittner is head of the Academy and deputy director of the Bauhaus Dessau Foundation. She is responsible for the conception and teaching of the postgraduate programmes for design, Bauhaus and architecture research. She curated numerous exhibitions on the Bauhaus and the cultural history of modernism. Her main areas of work include: international architectural and urban research, modernism and migration, the cultural history of modernism, and heritage studies. The results of her research and teaching have been widely published. She studied cultural studies and art history at the University of Leipzig and completed her PhD at the Institute for European Ethnology at the Humboldt-Universität zu Berlin. Since 2019, she has been an honorary professor at the Institute for European Art History and Archaeologies at Martin Luther University Halle-Wittenberg.

GUDSKUL

P. 17 is an educational knowledge-sharing platform formed in 2018 by the three Jakarta-based collectives *ruangrupa*, *Serrum* and *Grafis Huru Hara*. Gudskul sincerely believes in sharing and working together as two vital elements in developing Indonesian contemporary art and culture. Their intent is to disseminate initiative spirit through artistic and cultural endeavours in a society committed to collectivism, and to promote initiators who make local needs their highest priority, while at the same time contributing to and holding crucial roles internationally. Gudskul is building an ecosystem in which many participants are co-operating. This multiplicity contributes to diversifying the issues and actors involved in every collaborative project that happens within a social, political, cultural, economical, environmental and pedagogical context. Gudskul is open to anyone who is interested in co-learning, developing collective-based artistic practices, and art-making with a focus on collaboration.

KATJA KLAUS

P. 17 Katja Klaus is a research associate at the Academy of the Bauhaus Dessau Foundation, acting as deputy head of the department since 2018. Her work focuses on pedagogy, design and digital mediation. After obtaining a certificate of advanced studies as Digital Curator from Pausanio Academy, Cologne, in 2021, she has been responsible for the digital research project *Schools of Departure*, an online atlas of design and art education beyond the Bauhaus. Furthermore, Katja has been leading the development of online teaching modules in the context of the international *Bauhaus Open Studios* programme, a programme she has been heading since 2015. From 2005 to 2014, the media, theatre and pedadogy scholar (MA) worked as an advisor to the director of the Bauhaus Dessau Foundation.

PHILIPP SACK

19 P. 17 Philipp studied art history, modern history, and museology in Heidelberg, Lyon, and Paris. A researcher and educator in art, he is interested in pedagogical approaches emerging in the interplay between cultural and educational institutions, and in the history and theory of visual cultures. As part of his work at the nexus between research practice and institutional structures, he also is engaged with issues of transcultural education policy.

BA-BAU AIR

P. 37 ba-bau AIR (contemporarily) is an independent collective-run art residency, studio and kitchen located in the center of Hanôi, founded in January 2019. Focusing on the concept of *Duyên* (destined encounter), ba-bau connects, supports and incubates multi- and interdisciplinary collaborations. ba-bau AIR works as a medium, a safe space to host, cohabit, converse, and experiment not only with anything/anyone happening to the space but also with the concept of running the space itself.

PANGROK SULAP

P. 45 Pangrok Sulap is a Malaysian collective of artists, musicians and social activists with a mission to empower rural communities and the marginalised through art. *Pangrok* is the local pronunciation of 'punk rock', and *Sulap* is a hut or resting place usually used by farmers in Sabah, Borneo.
Since 2013, woodcut prints have become the collective's main tool in spreading social messages, through large-scale exhibition works as well as handmade merchandise including cloth badges, tote bags, t-shirt's and commissioned ban-

ners for events. The collective are strong advocates of the DIY concept, hence the slogan *Jangan Beli, Bikin Sendiri* ('Don't buy it, do it yourself'). The collective's work often focuses on retelling the narratives of Borneo's rural communities, of endangered ways of life, forests, flora and fauna. It captures light-hearted moments of human interaction and explores more hard-hitting contents such as human rights, political corruption and environmental exploitation. In the work created collectively by its numerous members, many hands create an aesthetically cohesive style and voice. Community participation is a strong part of Pangrok Sulap's process. The collective collaborates with community members to collate indigenous narratives and experiences and create artworks that tell their stories. Members of the public are encouraged to join in the communal production of art works and the printing process. Examples include a performance during which the collective plays original and contemporary folk music while participants are invited to dance in circles on the woodcut blocks performing the traditional *Sumazau* folk dance of Sabah. The crowd's weight transfers ink onto the finished print which is then revealed on the spot.

SALIKHAIN KOLEKTIB

P. 53 Salikhain Kolektib is an interdisciplinary collective based in the Philippines with a network in the Asia-Pacific region. The collective integrates art, research, education, and community engagement and development into various collaborative artworks and initiatives. The common ground for the members of Salikhain is the collective's interests in participatory art and research practices and the environment (salikhainkolektib.com).

BISHKEK SCHOOL OF CONTEMPORARY ART (BISCA)

P. 61 Diana Ukhina is a researcher, curator and artist who has been working as an independent cultural actor since 2010. She is a co-founder of the self-organised platform Bishkek School of Contemporary Art (BiSCA) (2020), chairwoman of Synergy Art Studio (2015), and a participant of the Central Asian art collective Davra (2022). She holds an MA in sociology from the American University of Central Asia and focuses on the sociology of culture. Her interests include art as a process and experience, the interweaving of cultural and sound memories, the art history of Kyrgyzstan, museums as public heritage, gender and the city, and the methodology of artistic research. She has implemented various research-based and museum exhibitions, educational artistic programmes, and research-based art projects. Oksana Kapishnikova is a curator, art historian and artist. She is a co-founder of BiSCA, an executive secretary of the National Committee of the International Council of Museums in Kyrgyzstan (2019) and a curator of the Museum of Feminist Art (2019). She earned her Master's degree in Museum Studies at the Higher School of Economics (Moscow, 2016 –2019). For more than seven years, she was employed at the Gapar Aitiev Kyrgyz National Museum of Fine Arts. She has worked on several museum exhibitions, arts exhibitions, research-oriented exhibitions and educational programmes. Alima Tokmergenova is a researcher, artist and editor. She is a co-founder of BiSCA and a member of the Synergy Art Studio. Her main themes and interests include the city, gender, craftivism and the art history of Kyrgyzstan. She has participated in various exhibitions, research projects and educational programmes. Ravshan Ta Jing is an architectural designer and artist. He is a co-founder of BiSCA, a designer in the architectural studio Tsarik Architecture, and a teacher at the Technical School of Innovation AUCA. He holds a degree in environmental design. His main interests include the city, gender and urbanism. He has participated in various exhibitions and educational programmes. Bermet Borubaeva is a researcher, curator and artist who has worked on environmental, gender and labour issues after completing her studies at the Contemporary Art School in Bishkek (2009). She is a co-founder of BiSCA and has participated in a number of regional and international art projects. She holds an MA in political science from the Higher School of Economics (Moscow) and focuses on the political economy of environmental pollution. Her interests include food, ecology, labour, equality, and urban studies. She has published extensively on art, political economics, migration and environmental justice. Kanaiym Kydyralieva is an artist, editor, educator and researcher. She is a co-founder of BiSCA. She earned her MSc in economics and management at the Humboldt-Universität zu Berlin. In addition to her artistic practice, she teaches data analysis and statistics to students of economics and business administration.

ANOTHER ROADMAP SCHOOL

P. 75 Another Roadmap School is the name of an international network of practitioners and researchers who are working toward art education as an engaged practice in museums, cultural institutions, educational centres and grassroots organisations in 22 cities on four continents. The Another Roadmap Africa Cluster (ARAC) comprises all of its working groups that are based in African cities. It is currently active in the cities of Kampala, Nyanza, Lubumbashi, Kinshasa, Maseru, Johannesburg, Lagos and Cairo. Founded in Uganda in 2015, the ARAC exists to foster Africa-based conversations about the arts and education, particularly with respect to colonialism's epistemological and aesthetic legacies. It aims to develop a shared knowledge base and a structure of mutual learning that is genuinely accessible to and meaningful for cultural workers on the continent.

The ARAC developed as localised and regional components of a collective research project concerned with the history of arts education, undertaken with a network of educators, artists and researchers working in four continents. It was initiated at the Institute for Art Education of Zurich University of the Arts (ZHdK). The working groups of the ARAC include members of the Keleketla! Library, Keep the Dream Arts, Wits School of Arts (University of the Witwatersrand) and independent cultural workers who compose the Johannesburg working group; the Kampala working group in Uganda, operating at Nagenda International Academy of Art & Design (NIAAD); the Lubumbashi working group, operating at Centre d'art Waza; the Nyanza working group in Rwanda, working from the former Nile Source Polytechnic of Applied Arts (NSPA); the Maseru working group in Lesotho, active at Ba re e ne re Literary Trust, and the Cairo working group in Egypt, hosted by the Contemporary Image Collective (CIC).

OLA UDUKU

P. 85 Ola Uduku is Head of Liverpool School of Architecture. Prior to this appointment she was Research Professor in Architecture at Manchester School of Architecture (2017 to 2021). From 2011 to 2017, she had been Reader in Architecture, and Dean for Africa, at Edinburgh University. Her research specialisms are in modern architecture in West Africa, the history of educational architecture in Africa, and contemporary issues related to social infrastructure provision for minority communities in the 'West' and 'South'. She is an advocate of equity in all its forms in the workplace, particularly in the architectural profession. She promotes the Documentation and recording of Modernist Buildings and Landscapes (Docomomo) Africa, and is a former President of the African Studies Association UK.

PEDRO J S VIEIRA DE OLIVEIRA

P. 95 Pedro J S Vieira de Oliveira (b.1985) is a Brazilian researcher, sound artist and educator living in Berlin. He is currently a fellow of the Junge Akademie der Künste Berlin under the programme *AI Anarchies*. He holds a PhD from Universität der Künste Berlin and is a founding member of the research platform Decolonising Design.

SUCHITRA BALASUBRAHMANYAN

P. 103 Suchitra Balasubrahmanyan (b.1964) is a design historian and visiting professor with research interests in nineteenth and twentieth century craft and design. She was a curatorial advisor in the *bauhaus imaginista* project, tracing the flows of design ideas and expertise in India against the backdrop of decolonisation, nationalism and Cold War diplomacy. Her current research is on 'modern' block printed textiles in western India and their adaptive response to contemporary issues and receptivity to global influences.

UNCONDITIONALDESIGN

P. 113 UnconditionalDesign is a design research project founded in 2017 as part of the ruangrupa Art Laboratory that aims to collect and study the phenomenon of informal design practices and urban innovation in Indonesia. UnconditionalDesign conducts participatory documentation and archiving through Instagram. This method has been successful in collecting hundreds of case samples from all over Indonesia over the past five years.

ASIA ART ARCHIVE (AAA)

P. 121 Asia Art Archive is an independent non-profit organisation initiated in 2000 in response to the urgent need to document the multiple recent histories of art in the region and to make

19

them accessible. With a valuable collection of materials on art freely available on their website and at their Hong Kong on-site library, AAA builds tools and communities to collectively expand knowledge through research, residency and educational programmes. Part of AAA's effort is to build a community that enriches conversations around art and function as an important resource and catalyst for scholarship in the field. They organise exhibitions, talks, workshops, publications, conferences, symposia and research grants for and with art professionals, educators, academics, artists and the interested public. Generosity is at the core of what AAA does—a desire to see work shared freely, ethically, and sustainably, benefiting as many people as possible.

19

LOAD NA DITO

P. 131 Load Na Dito (est. 2016) is an arts and research initiative based in Manila, Philippines. Developed as a homemade culture, it uses any available space as a site for knowledge-sharing, Inquiry, and discussion. Load Na Dito (meaning 'load now here') is a local top-up system for cellphone credit which you can use anywhere you see the sign. Developing this idea as a model, the Initiative creates projects in different locations, in various formats and sizes. By organising and co-organising a wide range of programmes, Load Na Dito hopes to critically address the questions of participation and collaboration in relation to the practice of contemporary art.

OMNIKOLEKTIF

P. 139 Established on April 16, 2015, Omnispace is a space organisation and collective that embodies art and alternative activities to support the young culture scene in Bandung. 'Omni' also refers to a Latin prefix meaning 'all' or 'every'. In 2021, Omnispace expanded its movement through Omnikolektif. From then on, it was not only running a physical space but was more concerned with collective practices. Located in Bandung, Indonesia, Omnikolektif is a contemporary art collective focusing on education, knowledge exchange, alternative ways of distribution of art and ideas. Their goal is to provide an inclusive space for actors in creative fields as well as for the general public to create an environment conducive to collaboration while considering the economic value needed to sustain the collective.

CHANGKYU LEE

Changkyu Lee is currently pursuing his PhD in anthropology at Binghamton State University of New York (SUNY). He received his MA in anthropology from Seoul National University where he completed a thesis entitled *Wayang Kulit Gaya Yogyakarta: Meaning and Transformation in Contemporary Indonesia* (2009). His research interests are anthropology of art, material culture, Islamic spirituality and the hierarchy of artistic value and aesthetics in the global art world. Currently, he is a member of the MVW (Material and Visual Worlds) working group at SUNY Binghamton.

SERRUM

Serrum is an art and education study group in Jakarta established in 2006. The word *Serrum* stands for 'sharing room'. Serrum focuses on educational, socio-political and urban issues with educational and artistic presentational approaches. The group's activities cover a wide array of activities such as art projects, exhibitions, workshops, creative discussions and propaganda. Serrum's mediums are video, murals, graphics, comics and installation art.

NINA PAIM

Nina Paim is an editor, designer, curator, and researcher based in Porto. Her work revolves around notions of directing, supporting, and collaborating. A three-time recipient of the Swiss Design Award, Nina has taught and lectured internationally. In 2020, she co-founded the feminist platform for design politics *Futuress,* which she currently co-directs alongside Maya Ober.

OFFSHORE

Offshore is a Zurich- and Eindhoven-based design studio, founded by Isabel Seiffert and Christoph Miler. Their projects focus on editorial design, typography, image-making, as well as research-driven visual narratives. Next to commissions, collaborations and self-initiated research, the duo engages in design education at various art schools within the Netherlands, Switzerland and Germany. The studio co-founded, co-edited and designed the publication series *Migrant Journal* and received the Swiss Design Award in Graphic Design in 2022. In

2020/21 the duo was in residence at the Jan van Eyck Academy and continued their visual research at the La Becque Artist Residency in 2022.

19

IMAGE CREDITS

1   Study collection of the National Institute of Design (NID), Ahmedabad, 2017. Photograph: Regina Bittner.

2   Kecoak Timur/Gudskul, Slametan opening ritual for Bauhaus Study Rooms, December 2020. Stiftung Bauhaus Dessau / Photo: Thomas Meyer, 2020 / OSTKREUZ.

3   Stages of resting, ba-bau AIR collective presentation in documenta fifteen, 2022. Still image from 'Untitled' (2022), Nguyễn Duy Anh. Picture credit/ jinpanji.

4   Pangrok Sulap, Wood cut 'Raikan rakyat' (Celebrate the people), 2017.

5   Documentary photograph by Kim Talavera, taken in the context of Salikhain Kolektib's workshop 'Art for Resilient Communities', Sulu-an Island, 2019.

6   Project documentation 'History of 20th century art in Kyrgyzstan in the practices of female artists', Gapar Aitiev Kyrgyz National Museum of Fine Arts, Bishkek, 2020.

7   Travelling printing kit in a suitcase, project at documenta fifteen, Kassel, 2022.

8   International School Ibadan. Photograph: Ola Uduku.

9   Escola Aberta, 2012. Photo by Radim Peško.

10 Low cost wheelchair with its designer, Shailendra Yagnik (Case 2 - Design for Health: A wheelchair for India). Photograph by Avinash Pasricha, 1978. Courtesy: Archives, National Institute of Design, Ahmedabad.

11 Unconditional design workshop documentation, 2020.

12 Jiang Zhuyun, Sound of Temperature, 2005, video; part of the installation Learning What Can't Be Taught, Asia Art Archive Library, 2021. Photo: Kitmin Lee.

13 MIL OBJETOS IT AKEAN (One Thousand Objects in Aklan) by Greys Lockheart in collaboration

with Northwestern Visayan Colleges, Aklan. Image courtesy of the artist

14	Omnikolektif, Climbing Ivy, 2022.
15	Omnikolektif, Climbing Ivy, 2022 (inverted).
16	PRESISI: Students in Maumere meet their locality learning resource.
17	Escola Aberta, 2012, photo by Radim Peško (inverted).
18	Portable split light table set up for stereo viewing, 1957. USDA Forest Service, Pacific Northwest Region, State and Private Forestry, Forest Health Protection. Photograph: W.C. Guy. https://archive.org/details/usdafs-36780098026, accessed 22 June 2023.

13

SCHOOLS OF DEPARTURE

#1 Decolonising design education
#2 The New Designer: Design as a profession
     All issues can be found under:
     atlas.bauhaus-dessau.de/en/journal

IMPRINT

The *Schools of Departure* series is published in connection with the homonymous online research platform, a digital atlas established by the Bauhaus Dessau Foundation with the objective to map experiments in art and design education beyond the Bauhaus. These experiments are understood as manifestations of travelling concepts which, with ever-shifting connotations, keep a wide variety of educational approaches in a process of constant exchange and motion. Studying these phenomena through the lens of travelling concepts such as Decolonisation, New Designers, New Communities, Creativity, Craft, Science, or Deschooling enables us to explore narratives around 'routes of appropriation' that move between different geographies, times and cultures.

This book aggregates a selection of texts that have initially been created for the online research platform in late 2022. It constitutes one of two inaugural issues of the series, with new volumes to appear on a yearly basis.

The online research platform *Schools of Departure* was partly funded in 2021 in the context of the Digital Agenda for the State of Saxony-Anhalt with funds from the Ministry of Infrastructure and Digital Affairs of the State of Saxony-Anhalt. In 2022, the project has been further developed as part of *dive in. Programme for Digital Interactions* of the Kulturstiftung des Bundes (German Federal Cultural Foundation) with funding by the Federal Government Commissioner for Culture and the Media (BKM) through the NEUSTART KULTUR programme.

atlas.bauhaus-dessau.de

Bauhaus Dessau Foundation
Gropiusallee 38
06846 Dessau-Roßlau
Germany
represented by:
Director and CEO
Barbara Steiner

Edited by
Regina Bittner, Katja Klaus,
Catherine Nichols, and Philipp Sack

Copy-editing
Philipp Sack

Proofing
Frederik Richthofen

Design
Offshore, (Isabel Seiffert and
Christoph Miler), offshorestudio.ch

Coding
Leonardo Angelucci, 0x000.ch

Printing and Binding
Gutenberg Beuys Feindruckerei
GmbH, Langenhagen

Publisher
Spector Books
Harkortstrasse 10, 04107 Leipzig
www.spectorbooks.com

Distribution
Germany, Austria: GVA,
    Gemeinsame
    Verlagsauslieferung
    Göttingen GmbH&Co. KG,
    www.gva-verlage.de
Switzerland: AVA
    Verlagsauslieferung AG,
    www.ava.ch
France, Belgium: Interart Paris,
    www.interart.fr
UK: Central Books Ltd,
    www.centralbooks.com
USA, Canada, Central and South
America, Africa: ARTBOOK/ D.A.P.,
    www.artbook.com
South Korea: The Book Society,
    www.thebooksociety.org
Japan: twelvebooks,
    www.twelve-books.com
Australia, New Zealand:
    Perimeter Distribution,
    www.perimeterdistribution.com

First Edition, 2023
Printed in Germany
© Bauhaus Dessau Foundation
ISBN 978-3-95905-747-9

The Bauhaus Dessau Foundation is
a non-profit foundation under public
law. It is institutionally funded by:

Die Beauftragte der Bundesregierung
für Kultur und Medien

SACHSEN-ANHALT

#moderndenken

Dessau
⌐ Roßlau